CHRISTIAN

Audrey Beslow

ABINGDON PRESS/N

SEX AND THE SINGLE CHRISTIAN

This book is printed on acid-free paper.

Library of Congress Cataloging-in-Publication Data

BESLOW, AUDREY, 1931–
  Sex and the single Christian.
  1. Single people—Religious life. 2. Middle age—Religious life.
  3. Single people—Sexual behavior. 4. Middle age—Sexual behavior.
  5. Celibacy. 6. Chastity I. Title.
  BV4596.S5B47   1987   241'.66   86-17262

ISBN 0-687-38197-5 (alk. paper)

BOOK DESIGN BY JOHN ROBINSON

Scripture quotations in this publication unless otherwise noted are from the
Revised Standard Version of the Bible, copyrighted 1946, 1952, © 1971, 1973
by the Division of Christian Education of the National Council of the
Churches of Christ in the U.S.A., and are used by permission.

The Scripture quotation marked NIV (page 131) is from the Holy Bible, New
International Version. Copyright © 1973, 1978, 1984, International Bible
Society.

MANUFACTURED BY THE PARTHENON PRESS
NASHVILLE, TENNESSEE, UNITED STATES OF AMERICA

ACKNOWLEDGMENTS

*T*o my pastors, Lloyd Ogilvie, Ralph Osborne, Jack Loo, and Rob Norris for their encouragement and critiques. To Rick Sullivan, Arlene Clarke, and the Birthday Club—Genny Faulstich, Karin Elliott-Chandler, and Nancy Milei—for faithfully supporting me and giving me careful feedback throughout the entire five-year process. To Jo Gifford, Doris Burke, Phyllis Hart, Libby Patterson, Bill Ricketts, Janet Laughter, Bob Parker, Gary Bausman, Dick Elliott-Chandler, and members of the Pasadena Writers' Guild—Warren Brown, Clint McLemore, and Val Toms—for their ideas and critiques. To people from Serendipity Singles and Single Spirit of Hollywood Presbyterian Church and the other singles' groups whose sharing of their lives and questions have contributed to this book. To my cousins, Jacqueline and Charles Krum, who encouraged me through the hard times of my own singleness. And to all the men and women over the past twenty years whose conversations and experiences have helped to shape this book—thank you.

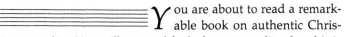

You are about to read a remarkable book on authentic Christian sexuality. You will not read far before you realize that this is no bland reiteration of religious rules and regulations. Nor is it a theoretical analysis of the sexual behavior of the growing single population in America. And it is not an aloof lip-smacking exposé of the fears and frustrations of singles as they struggle to deal with their sexuality.

Instead, you are in for a vital encounter with a joyous, life-affirming person who has some courageous convictions about how to live as a single with love and fulfillment. With an amazing combination of sensitivity and empathy as well as hard-hitting frankness, Audrey Beslow writes as a single to singles about a secret she has discovered and lived. Drawing on her immense experience as an educator, counselor, social analyst, and church lay leader, she movingly describes Christian sexuality, which is rooted in reverence and responsibility.

Audrey Beslow sounds a clarion call for intimacy and celibacy. Both words, and the true quality of life they denote, are badly misinterpreted and misused today. They seem mutually exclusive, because we think of intimacy as sexual intercourse and celibacy as an exceptional religious vow.

Not so. Intimacy with God and others of both sexes, married and single, is the deep longing of all of us. The myth is that marriage and intercourse automatically provide this intimacy. This not only accounts for the preoccupation with sex and the longing for marriage among many singles, but also is a major cause of the escalating divorce rate. True intimacy, to use Audrey Beslow's words, is "based on complete trust, openness, and willingness to share one's feelings totally." With incisive clarity and gripping illustrations, she reveals how singles can find this truly satisfying intimacy with God, and in profound friendships with the opposite sex that need not lead to either sexual intercourse or marriage.

The key to wholeness and health in intimacy for a single, according to Audrey Beslow, is surprisingly a commitment to celibacy. She gives the finest definition and explanation of celibacy as a gift of God I have ever read. It is both life-affirming and liberating. Most of all, it makes possible a natural, relaxed, unstudied enjoyment of others as persons and not as things to be used. Here is a positive alternative to our "thinging-it" culture, in which "I-thou" respect and caring is replaced by "It-it" opportunism. In contrast, Audrey Beslow describes a healthy single life-style and presents a framework of beliefs that enables a person to live the single life to the fullest. She calls singles to wholeness, adventure, and service in the here and now, rather than waiting, searching, and longing for a mate.

Of significance is that Audrey Beslow lives the wholesome life she describes. I have known Audrey for fifteen years as a friend and one of her pastors. She has served as an elder, church school teacher, and visionary leader. Audrey has the gift of wisdom. She is committed to excellence and has that "Why not?" enthusiasm for God's best for herself, her friends, and her church. As a disciplined student of the Bible, she brings a biblical perspective to all that she says and does. A person of prayer, she lives life with resilience and gusto.

It is my privilege to introduce this outstanding Christian leader to you and to commend for your enrichment this benchmark book. It is a must for every single. The book is an excellent and effective resource for a church school class, small group discussion, and retreats or conferences. It should also be required reading for pastors and church leaders. And for everyone, single or married, it prompts a reexamination of his or her belief system that controls the use or misuse of the awesome gift of sexuality.

Lloyd John Ogilvie
Senior Pastor
First Presbyterian Church
of Hollywood

CONTENTS

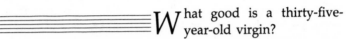

What good is a thirty-five-year-old virgin?

This question arises naturally from today's culture. The overwhelming majority of modern popular songs and screenplays contain one basic assumption: that young men and women will not only seek sexual experience, they will (if they are reasonably assertive and even marginally intelligent) attain it. People who pass the age of thirty, twenty-seven, twenty-four, even twenty-one without experiencing the mysteries of sex are considered foolish. To be sexually uninitiated, in a society that makes sex so available and publicizes it so highly, takes great naiveté—or else it takes great discipline and strong reasons to endure this discipline.

Is your relationship going anywhere? is another common question asked of men and women who have been seeing each other for awhile. This implies that all male-female relationships should be romantically or erotically based and if the friendship is not progressing toward one of these goals, it is time to move on. The idea of friendship between men and women that isn't leading toward either sex or marriage seems as foolish to many as the thought of celibacy.

However, some people do spend their time of singleness very richly as celibates—that is, abstaining from sexual intimacy—and have meaningful friendships with people of the other sex. Why and how they do so form the framework of this book.

Our society, especially the Protestant church, generally sees singleness as a problem and marriage as the solution, but this does not seem to be the way Jesus looked at relationships. Although the apostle Peter and perhaps other disciples of Jesus were married, some were probably single. Marital status was so unimportant that in four biographies of Jesus' travels, only Peter's marriage is mentioned, and then only because of the illness of his mother-in-law. Although the women traveling with Jesus and the disciples (named in Luke 8:2, 3) were both married and single, marital status seems to have made no difference. Jesus, himself single, seemed to enjoy spending time in the home of his single friends in Bethany—Martha, Mary, and Lazarus—and no one seemed to push any of these singles to marry. Looking at Jesus' friends and life-style, it seems unlikely that he would be as concerned about marital status as we are in the church today.

Christian Thinking Is Changing

Since singles, secular and Christian, spend considerable time and energy on sex and marriage—pursuing, discussing, fantasizing, or avoiding—our attitudes and beliefs about these two subjects play a major role in how healthy we can become.

In the mid-1900s, most Christians would have agreed that sex for singles was wrong because the King James version of the Bible translated the Greek word *porneia* as "fornication," and the English dictionary told us that *fornication* meant sexual intercourse between unmarried persons. The issue was clear.

Modern translations use "immorality" for the word *porneia* since the Greek means various kinds of gross sexual sins. In our society, even among many Christians, sex between consenting adults is not considered a gross sexual sin. So the rules are not as clearly defined today as they appeared to be thirty years ago.

Lewis Smedes, however, has presented an excellent case for single celibacy from the positive viewpoint of what sex is intended to be, in his book *Sex for Christians* (Eerdmans, 1976). So the loss of a distinct negative does not give us license to do what we want; it simply raises more questions. What does Scripture mean by "immoral"? How did God create us to operate best?

Christian Action Is Changing

My experience in speaking and counseling indicates that many Christian singles, even in conservative churches, are sexually active. Some of these are leaders, confident people who think for themselves; they simply do not believe that abstinence is meant for them. Other singles are fearful of losing out because their underlying belief system tells them that to be celibate is to be cheated. Since sex is on a pedestal in America, almost everything we hear in both the secular world and the church tells us that we should expect sexual fulfillment. The world's answer is to find a consenting partner, whereas the church's instruction is to get married. Many Christian singles simply leave the church so that they won't be faced with the tension or guilt of an unacceptable life-style; others simply keep quiet.

New Thinking Needed for Middle-aged Singles

Middle-aged singles (35-55) as a major group in society and the church are a fairly new phenomenon. The church is trying to apply its old framework developed for teenagers—deny yourselves, take cold showers, and try to find a spouse—for all Christian singles, old and young. Until quite recently, almost all books published about singles either stressed how to find a mate or, possibly, how to endure. Recent additions emphasize how to be healed from divorce or widowhood, which seems to be the current focus of "singles' ministries" in the church. These views interpret singleness as a time of waiting, healing, hoping, and looking for the next mate. The implication is that all successful singles find a spouse.

We Need to Discuss Sex

Where sex is not openly discussed in adult Christian community, each confused or disillusioned single seeks his or her own way without model or guideline from a Christian

11

perspective. I'm convinced that we all hold erroneous views about men, women, sex, and God without understanding which of our views are inaccurate.

One major purpose of this book is to stimulate discussion in the church on the topics of sex and celibacy. I have accordingly included discussion questions, which are set apart in boxes at the ends of various sections of the book. These may be used in a formal classroom situation, such as a Sunday school class, or in a less formal setting. The questions are purposely open-ended—that is, they do not have one correct answer—in order to stimulate the kind of discussion in which our personal views can begin to surface and be challenged.

Those who are celibate, especially, need to be able to articulate a reason for remaining celibate both for their own sake and for the encouragement of others, since it is not easy to stay celibate in today's world. Understanding the beliefs that underlie specific behavior—our own and others'—is valuable in learning to love, in accepting our own sexuality, and in knowing God, because he made of us sexual beings.

It is imperative that we as Christians explore the ways in which our sexuality contributes to full and healthy lives for singles. It is my hope that this book will aid that exploration.

Some Important Questions

I have been closely involved with singles over the past twenty-five years as a counselor, as a friend, as a teacher, and as a single myself. I have lived in coed dorms and in apartments for singles, and have kept ties with several groups of secular and Christian singles over a period of years. This has given me some insight into the effects of different sexual life-styles, the disparity between the traditional stand of the church and the reality of what is happening among singles today, and some ways in which healthy singles have developed satisfying life-styles and ministries. These experiences have raised in my mind three important questions, which we will be exploring in this book.

Question One: What Are the Consequences of Sexual Union?

My curiosity about this subject began about twenty years ago, when a seventh-grade girl stayed after school in my classroom day after day moaning that everyone in her crowd had "made it" with a boy except her. How, she asked, could she find a boy who would "make it" with her?

I wondered what I could tell her about her goal. Were there consequences beyond pregnancy and venereal disease for a girl who started sexual intimacy with boys at age thirteen? School gave her information about the physical results of sexual union, but could I tell her anything factual about the psychological effects? If she were properly protected against pregnancy and V.D., would there be any damage to her if she continued the sexual pattern she was choosing?

(Interestingly, twenty years have made a change in society's knowledge of the physical effects of sexual intercourse. In the early sixties, people thought humanity had reached a new level of sexual freedom. "The pill" and penicillin magically made sex available to anyone without the old intimidators of pregnancy and V.D. that had held back previous generations of middle-class women. That was before side effects to "the pill" were discovered and before nature created new strains of venereal disease immune to penicillin—and to any other medicine currently known. This was also before researchers made the connection between cervical cancer and the number of sex partners a woman has. So we are not as free from physical consequences as it looked in the early sixties. What else may be discovered?)

My frustration in feeling that this young girl was going to hurt herself, but not knowing how or why or what to say to someone from a nonreligious home where premarital sex was an accepted way of life led me to consider the first question with which this book deals: *Are there psychological consequences of sexual union that are not immediately observable, which at some future time may limit choices and relationships?*

This question was reinforced as I observed the life-styles of the singles in my apartment building. Were those who felt no

13

claim of God on their lives free to do as they pleased sexually without any negative consequences to their lives?

Question Two: Is Celibacy Best?

Christian singles approach the decision about sexual actions from a set of beliefs about God and about sex that often surface only when we discuss our desires, fears, and experiences. Repeatedly I heard uncertainties expressed by Christians:

- single celibates in their late thirties and forties wondering what difference it would make if they satisfied their curiosity about sex now, since "ideal" marriage and family has probably passed them by.
- singles believing that God could not possibly expect mature adults to abstain from sexual activity since they assumed that no one can be whole and healthy without continued sexual intercourse.
- men and women needing to reassure themselves of their masculinity or femininity by whatever kind of sexual experience that would achieve this desire.
- Christian divorcés wondering if their marriages would have been better if they or their spouses had had practice as a lover with others before marriage.

These and many more concerns of Christians reaffirmed my interest in the question of the more-than-physical effects of sex on a person. I wondered if there might be valid reasons for a difference in behavior between young singles and older singles, and if the Bible had anything to say specifically to older singles in situations like ours. If there were other valid options, we should hear about them in a Christian setting. This need for information led me to my second question: *Is God's highest good and most loving plan for all singles that we abstain from sexual intercourse as long as we are single, or is there an alternative?*

Question Three: What Is a Healthy Life-style?

Hundreds of singles are active in the church I attend, but when a pastor was hired to begin a work for singles, many of us resisted committing ourselves to this ministry. Since we had already been integrated into the mainstream of the church, the idea of serving just singles seemed like a step backward. All of us identified more as persons, as Christians, as women or men, and as members of our various professions and ministries than we identified as singles. Although singles' groups are needed for social activities and to help new singles, healthy Christian singles seem to be either mainstreamed in the church or banded together for ministry.

The potential for wholeness, power, service, and adventure for singles today is fantastic. What a terrible waste that many singles spend so many years waiting, searching, and longing for a mate, rather than living wholesomely in the here and now.

Healthy, active singles need—and I believe God intends—a better framework than merely waiting, merely preparing for marriage. Singleness is a time for risking, growing, and living richly in ways that are not possible during marriage. We need to talk about exciting life-styles for single Christians, and explore how sexuality and our need for intimacy fit into these life-styles. Christian singleness needs a new image. This desire to present a wholesome view of singleness has led to the third question: *What does a healthy, single life-style look like?*

Looking for Answers

In the first part of this book we will explore some tentative answers to the first two questions, What are the effects of sex? and, Is celibacy God's best? We will examine various sexual life-styles as to their rightness as Christian options, using criteria found in scripture—particularly the test of love, since God's command to us is that we love. Then we will examine the effects of sexual activity, the characteristics of sex and celibacy, some reasons singles pursue sex or celibacy, and the need for healing.

In the second part we will consider the question of what a healthy, single life-style might look like. I will present a framework of beliefs and ways to structure time and relationships, a framework that will be useful as we seek to live the single life to its fullest.

QUESTIONS FOR THOUGHT AND DISCUSSION

1. What are the differences between the beliefs about marriage and sex of a twenty-year-old single and those of a forty-year-old single?

2. What concerns about sex do you hear from Christian singles?

3. How do men or women who have never married differ from the divorced in sexual expectations and perceived sexual needs?

4. Are the consequences of sex outside of marriage different for Christians and non-Christians?

Evaluating a Life-style

This book is written with the philosophy that we are created beings and therefore operate best in the way the Creator intended us to function. Had we evolved, then whatever seemed to work at the moment would be our only criterion for choosing ways to live. Evolved beings have no standard of what is better except each individual's judgment. No plumbline to evaluate life exists in a world without a Creator; each person's guess is as valid as another's. But if we accept as a baseline a caring Creator who has revealed himself to his created beings, then we do have a valid criterion against which to measure the helpfulness, validity, or reasonableness of behavior: the test of his revealed truth, the Scripture, and particularly the test of love.

For the Christian, the Bible is the clearest expression of God's intent for humankind. I have long believed that the laws of God are true for all humans and that the relational principles of the Bible act as an instruction manual showing how humans operate optimally. God's physical laws work for everybody, not just for Christians, and they work whether we believe in them or not, as a two-year-old "Superman" will discover if he ignores the laws of gravity and steps out of a window to fly. I believe that there are also emotional-relational precepts that work the same for all of us, and that they too are ordained by God. Although the Bible's instructions are spiritual, where they clearly state principles in the physical or relational realms, they must be true for all people. Therefore we can and must consider life-styles according to biblical principles.

Love

The two great commandments given by Moses and affirmed by Jesus are, "You shall love the Lord your God with all your heart, and with all your soul, and with all your mind," and "You shall love your neighbor as yourself" (Matt. 22:37-39). In both these commandments the love referred to is the kind called *agape* ("ah-*gah*-pay") in Greek. We will consider what this kind of love means in greater detail in chapter 1; for now, however, let it suffice to say that agape involves selflessly devoting oneself to the one loved and contributing to that person's welfare.

To find God's highest and best plan for us, we must grow in our ability to exercise agape-love, both toward God and toward our neighbor. To discuss the relationship of singleness to one's love for the Lord would require another book; indeed, many books have been and are being written about the ways a person can develop his or her love for God.

17

(For the moment, let me simply point out the greater flexibility a single person has to use his or her time to develop this love, and that such love always shows itself in an increased obedience to Scripture.) Our focus, however, is on the second commandment: exercising agape toward our neighbor.

God's plan is that we aim our lives toward wanting the highest and best for the other, desiring the spiritual growth of ourselves and our neighbor, and extending ourselves in empathy, caring, patience, and other manifestations of agape-love. To allow ourselves to use people, to cause harm to people, or to relate without empathy, caring, or patience toward a person with whom we spend one-on-one time would be to ignore God's plan for our lives.

Therefore, considering each choice of sexual expression in view of the love it produces is important. Our ability to see the total picture of love—for God, for our neighbor, for ourselves—is too limited for our perception of love to be a conclusive test of morality, but applying the definition of agape-love to our experiences does eliminate some situations as being definitely opposed to love.

Adultery

In some instances the Bible is very clear about what is harmful to us. Where the Creator has clearly detailed his plan for us in negative terms, we see what his highest and best for us is *not*. One such negative is adultery.

The scripture is very clear about adultery in the Ten Commandments (Exod. 20:14) and by Jesus' affirmation of the commandment against adultery in Matthew 5:27-30. For a single to become involved with a married person in the sex act is specifically against God's plan. It is not just the married person who has committed a harmful act; the single person has intruded into a legal, emotional, willful, and spiritual vow. This is clearly not the good that God intends for his people.

We have all known people who have suffered through these affairs, even people who have eventually married, leaving a trail of hurt, scars, and dishonor to God's name.

18

Thank God for forgiveness, cleansing, redemption, and a fresh start, but we know that adultery is off limits before we become involved in it.

Immorality

Paul makes lists of sins—those actions and thoughts contrary to God's nature and will—in most of his letters (Gal. 5:19, Eph. 5:5, Col. 3:5, etc.). The lists include the sexual sins of immorality, impurity, evil desire, and licentiousness. These seemed to be gross sexual sins obviously wrong in those societies and often connected with temple worship of heathen gods. Immorality, according to the *Random House Dictionary*, is synonymous with being "depraved," or "wicked." Many people would not accept sex between two consenting singles as falling into this definition. The same dictionary defines *licentious* as being "sexually unrestrained." Again, most sexually active singles have some kind of moral constraints determining limits on their sexual freedom. Therefore, even though many Christians accept the word *immorality*, translated as "fornication" in the King James version, as sufficient evidence that copulation for singles is not acceptable to God, some Christians do not believe that these lists define sex between consenting single adults in today's society as wrong.

What Is Helpful?

A helpful passage for me in clarifying God's ideal is 1 Corinthians 6:12-20. The idea here is that we measure our life-styles not by a legal code, but by what is helpful to the Christian walk, that which will not enslave us to any bodily desire. This rules out "sex as a fix" (which we will consider in chapter 2) for a Christian, since a "fix" has an enslaving power.

A Spiritual Bond

Paul states that the body belongs to God and that the Holy Spirit in the believer makes the body the temple of the Holy

Spirit. Paul's interpretation of the sex act is that joining one's body sexually to that of another person is to make the two one body, even if that other person is a prostitute. This recalls the statement in Genesis 2:24 that the goal of the marriage relationship, with its sexual union, is "one flesh"—physically, emotionally, and volitionally. Dr. Lewis Smedes states in *Sex for Christians:*

> The reality of the act [sexual intercourse], unfelt and unnoticed by them, is this: it unites them—body and soul—to each other. It unites them in that strange, impossible to pinpoint sense of "one flesh." There is no such thing as casual sex, no matter how casual people are about it.

One of the characteristics of God is integrity—that is, being integrated or all of one piece: consistent. Since God's intent for us is that we become like God by reflecting his character, anything that divides us or reduces our integrity is contrary to his will for us. For a Christian to join his or her body to another without accepting the volitional bonding that God has declared—that is, the commitment of marriage—is disintegrating. Every time we join ourselves to someone with whom we have no intent of making a permanent, complete bond, we are living a lie. Since God is truth and we are to be like him, there is no place to deliberately live a lie in the Christian life.

---

1. What are the implications of "one flesh" for those who have had more than one sex partner?
2. How do you interpret the words Paul uses for sexual sins in Galatians 5, Ephesians 5, Colossians 3, and Romans 1?
3. Why is love not a conclusive criterion for us to determine God's highest plan for our own lives?
4. What commands of Scripture can you think of that have been accepted by secular society as healthy principles for human interaction?

Examples and Terms

All case studies used in this book are real and verified by the experience of at least one person in addition to my original source. However, I have thoroughly disguised the characters because of the sensitivity of this subject. In my first drafts, when I used real experiences with only name and location changes, friends were incorrectly identifying themselves and others; this verified the commonality of the experiences, but also made me very cautious. To preserve the peace of mind of my friends and the people whom I interviewed, I have made composites of all characters except those who now have no connection with me and are therefore safe. Two characters, Frannie and Tom, are presented in different settings to illustrate some common patterns of those who remain single over a number of years.

Throughout this book I will be using the words *sex* (have sex, sex act, and so on), *lover, bed,* and *sleep with* to indicate sexual intercourse because these terms seem to communicate best to most people. The terms *sexuality* and *sexual expression* will be used to indicate the whole maleness or femaleness of a person. For example, celibacy is a form of sexual expression.

Objectives

My hope is that this book will:

1. Stimulate discussion among singles and those working with singles in churches so that each one's belief system motivating sexual behavior will be brought closer to the reality and truth of how God has created us.

2. Give singles some reasons to be celibate beyond idealism, fear, and blind obedience.

3. Give singles the freedom to state their desires to abstain without feeling abnormal.

4. Give singles confidence to enjoy the full advantage of singleness in relationships and ministry.

5. Encourage acceptance of singles by the church in their sexual journey toward wholeness.

21

This book is written especially for Christian singles who have felt the pull and influence of the secular world on their thinking, and for those who want to understand the thinking of singles. The subject of sex and singles needs to be more than just right or wrong. We need to discover what information singles need in order to make wise choices, and what encouragement is most helpful to singles in different circumstances. I offer this book toward these ends.

=1=
HOW BELIEF SYSTEMS DETERMINE CHOICES

Why does a person choose to have sexual intercourse outside of marriage? Why does another person choose to be celibate until marriage or after marriage is ended? Our choice of sexual involvement depends on our internalized belief about many subjects, including:

- Masculinity–femininity
- The effects of sex–need for sex–pleasure of sex
- God's love–God's judgment–God's view of sex

We have been absorbing these beliefs and other assumptions and fears from our families and surroundings since birth. The way we become aware of our assumptions and can begin to evaluate them as accurate or faulty is to observe our own behavior and the behavior of others, asking, What belief caused that behavior? Is that belief accurate according to the reality of how human beings are created? Sometimes we can see the fallacy or accuracy of a belief, but other times we must wait for further information.

Example of Belief Affecting Action: Mary and Bob

Mary's flirting had become a major issue between her and her fiancé, Bob.

"Why do you do it?" Bob ranted when they left the party. "You act like a whore!"

Mary raised her eyebrows. That was very strong language for Bob. Maybe she had gone too far.

23

"And wipe that smile off your face!" Bob continued.

Mary hadn't been aware of the smile, but she did feel good. She had had admiring attention from men, so Bob must have seen that she was attractive. Her mother had repeatedly told her, "To keep a man, you must continually make him see that other men are attracted to you." Mary didn't care that they had left the party early because she really wanted to be with Bob. She was pleased by his anger because it proved that he cared. Believing she had done what was necessary at the party to demonstrate to Bob her worth, she snuggled closer to him in the car.

"Get away!" Bob shouted.

Wow, he is angry, Mary thought. She had proved how attractive she was; what more could she do? She didn't want to lose him. Bob, however, believed that once a commitment is made neither partner should show any interest in another of the opposite sex. And he was now convinced that Mary was incapable of commitment.

These are conscious beliefs that an honest conversation could reveal. Correcting the situation would depend on how deeply each belief is rooted. Even if they attempt to accept the inaccuracy of their beliefs, Mary and Bob may fall back on the old tenets whenever they feel threatened.

Conflicting Beliefs

Most of us not only act on beliefs we have not verbalized to ourselves, we also hold conflicting beliefs without realizing it. A man may have accepted his church's teaching that God will only bless a marriage if both partners are celibate until the wedding night. But he may also have been impressed with stories "proving" that a man should be sexually experienced before marriage in order to make sex more pleasant for his wife. Unless he recognizes both beliefs and determines which belief has more validity for him, he will be uncomfortable with either choice.

This, of course, is an oversimplification because the motivating assumptions are often not verbalized and are so interrelated with other beliefs, fears, and needs that the resulting action is hard to trace. For example, the strength of his view of God as forgiving or judging could balance the choice. His fear of not being able to perform sexually or his need to please may also be entwined.

Mary's and Bob's example, and others in this book, are not given to excuse behavior or to confuse responsibility. The consequences of inaccurate belief systems always show up. Rather, the examples are given to encourage us to examine the truth of our assumptions as we discuss our fears and desires, and as we review our own behavior.

---

1. List statements about sex before marriage that you have read or heard, and consider the validity of each one.
2. Consider the sexual action that would result from each belief.
3. Roleplay Mary and Bob as they continue their discussion.
4. List other fears that affect sexual behavior.

Love: Eros or Agape

A vital part of our belief systems is our interpretation of what love is, since our language includes in the word *love* an entire spectrum of attitudes, including sexual passion, affection, goodwill, friendship, and a variety of other feelings and choices—emotions and acts of the will. In speaking of love, and in clarifying what happens in sexual relationships, it is important to have a clear understanding of the terms *eros* and *agape*.

Eros

I will use *eros* as M. Scott Peck defines it in his book *The Road Less Traveled* (Simon & Schuster, 1978), to mean mating instinct, the desire to merge with another being in order to assuage loneliness. The desire for sexual mating is always a part of eros. Because the drive stems from the need to obliterate one's own loneliness by this merger, eros is of necessity selfish. With that driving desire for the other person comes the wish to trap the partner so that loneliness will be banished forever. Eros initially is such a wonderful feeling that it is easy to become hooked on it—not wanting the work that builds a lasting relationship, the hard work of agape.

Eros lasts from six to thirty months, according to Peck. One reason that eros cannot last indefinitely is that the individuality of each person will eventually assert itself. She will want to make love and he will expect dinner on the table. He wants to go to the movies while she chooses to wash her hair. So each becomes aware again of being a separate entity.

Eros can be prolonged if it is unfulfilled. Because romantic love in the days of chivalry was worshipful and nonsexual, never fulfilled bodily, it could go on for a lifetime. If the love is one-sided, the lover always grasping but never feeling assured, eros may last indefinitely also. The mistress who spends her youth waiting for her lover to divorce exemplifies this eros. But eros satisfied is limited in time. Elements of agape must take over or the relationship will end.

Sheldon Vanauken in the biography of his marriage, *A Severe Mercy* (Harper & Row, Publishers, 1980), writes of his and his wife's attempt to keep their two lives completely merged throughout their marriage. Each tried to read everything the other had ever read, see everything the other had ever seen, even keep likes and dislikes the same. They made intricate rules to keep this merger and sameness intact. Peck, in *The Road Less Traveled*, describes falling in love (the merger the Vanaukens' marriage was trying to maintain) as temporary, selfish, a regression, and actually opposed to love because it inhibits growth. The elements of the Vanaukens' marriage described in the book, emphasizing the eros element of wanting total merger, appeared to be an inhibiting factor to their individual growth.

Agape

Agape, in contrast to eros's selfishness, is wanting the highest and best for another. Agape stems from the will, not the emotions, and is an action to nurture spiritual growth in oneself or another. Agape does not demand response as eros does, but can take pleasure in the beloved's growth as a separate being. Agape can rejoice in the beloved's achievements, but pure eros is competitive and fearful of losing the lover's attention. Agape allows the loved one freedom to grow and explore, but eros manipulates and dominates the lover, wanting to be involved in every aspect of the partner's life.

Many marriages and almost all long-term sex alliances are initially based on eros, and when eros dies, some marriages and most live-ins dissolve. But with many marriages and a few live-ins, because the will has made a commitment and the couple has at least considered the possibility of sickness, financial problems, in-law crises, or home and work conflicts, the individuals may choose to activate some of the qualities of agape—empathy, kindness, patience, endurance, or forgiveness—so that agape can temper some of the selfishness of eros.

Summary: Eros, Agape, and Love

Briefly, then, eros is sex-oriented, pleasure-centered, and selfish—an attempt to merge oneself into another being in order to escape the essential aloneness of existence. Agape is other-oriented, giving, unselfish, desirous of the other's growth, and can only be given if one has first received it from another. These are the two extremes of love, which few of us practice; between are the less extreme elements—companionship, mind-friend, and soul intimacy—which will be discussed in chapter 9. With these differences in mind, we can examine the kinds of relationships singles experience, interpreting the rationales behind and effects of each.

---

1. Give examples of the selfishness of eros from couples you have known.
2. Why did God create eros?

3. How would male-female relations be different if only agape-love were present?

4. Would non-eros dating be desirable?

5. Using Paul's list of agape's characteristics in 1 Corinthians 13:4-8, list an opposite for each of the positive qualities of love. How does each of these relate to eros?

6. List an opposite for each of the eight negative statements recorded in Paul's passage. How do these relate to love?

Sex Is in the Mind

Before we go further, we need to consider an important fact that is crucial to a healthy belief system: *Our bodies do not drive us to sexual intercourse. Our minds choose that course.*

Orgasm, obviously, is an intense, almost mindless experience. Even before orgasm, somewhere in the course of petting, a woman's body takes over from her mind and she has less and less control. But consider the difference in effect if a woman's breasts were touched by her lover, accidentally by a stranger in a crowded elevator, by a child, or by someone malicious. Would her body react the same? Or does her mind (her perception of the intent, the appropriateness of the place, the desirability of the person) control her body's reaction?

Even when the body has been turned on, a change in the mind's focus can change the body's response.

Examples of Sex in the Mind

A woman and her fiancé are lying on the couch together in front of the TV. Passion is increasing in its usual rhythm until the woman suddenly realizes that her lover's body is no longer responding. She pulls back to learn what has happened and finds him absorbed in the TV program. His mind has shifted and his body has responded to that shift.

A common example of the mind's role in sex is illustrated by another woman who leans back contentedly as she relaxes against the pillow, her body sated after an intense orgasm. Her husband begins touching her breasts in the same way that has earlier been so sensually desirable, but now it merely irritates her. She doesn't want to be turned on again; it's time to fix breakfast.

Our minds determine the body's responses.

The Mind Controls Our Sexual Actions

Our minds are even more in control in the decisions made before body contact. Most stimuli come through the eyes, especially for men; therefore, we can control what we look at. Another stimulus comes from memories and anticipations, pictures and feelings already in the mind. Although these images may float spontaneously into the mind, we can choose to dwell on them or to shift our thoughts. That desire that comes from the hormones when the body is "turned on" comes into the mind, and, although the body may have begun a response, by quickly occupying the mind with another subject the body's response can subside. This is exemplified by every junior-high boy who has learned to control his body by some trick of thinking for fear of being embarrassed in class. Once that control is learned, a man knows when he can allow himself to fantasize and when to switch his focus. The mind, therefore, is the crucial factor in dealing with sex drive.

Jesus, as recorded in Matthew 5:21-30, equated anger with murder and lust with adultery, indicating that what goes on in the mind is the forerunner of what the body does, and counts equally.

The more occupied our minds are with true caring for people, with achieving our goals, with beauty, truth, projects, and communing with God, the less our bodies will become aroused sexually. However, training the mind to shift its focus from sex to some other interest can be a slow process if fear is not the motivator. One does not necessarily achieve the desire to control one's mind in a month or even in a year.

29

Attaining a celibate mind takes discipline, but the result is great freedom in friendships. Tamiko is an example of a single with a celibate mind.

Tamiko the Friend

During Tamiko's teenage years the table tennis area in the recreation room had been a meeting place for the neighborhood boys and girls, as well as the church crowd. Tamiko considered boys as friends to beat at table tennis as well as to listen to. When the neighbor boy's girlfriend broke up with him, she sympathized as a caring friend, even though she was hoping that he might consider her his new girl. As each guy in the crowd bought a new stereo, got a job, or received his first car, Tamiko was the one to share it with because she asked the right questions and seemed genuinely enthused. In Bible studies, Tamiko considered the young men thinking people and she contributed equally, not playing games by pretending to be ignorant; in singing groups, she considered boys equal partners.

During her college years Tamiko had hiking buddies and opera friends, men who would work on her car in exchange for a meal and men who called just to chat and to share. When she became interested in someone romantically, it was often one of her male friends who would set up an opportunity for a date. Many of her male friends she had dated somewhere along the line, but honesty with genuine interest and caring had kept friendships when the romance died away.

After college, she found her habit of friendship extending to married men. For Tamiko this was not different from befriending the boys in the neighborhood she had grown up with when they were dating other girls. Rather than believing "All's fair in love and war," Tamiko accepted married men as totally off limits to even think about romantically. While Tamiko was visiting her mother one summer, a married male friend visiting in town without his wife came to her mother's house to pick Tamiko up for a day at the beach. Her mother was shocked. "You can't go out with a married man," she exclaimed to Tamiko.

"He's a friend, Mother. His wife is my friend, too," Tamiko explained. Her mother, however, remained unconvinced, not understanding how a man and a woman could be friends with no romantic interest.

Tamiko discovered that because her romances were celibate, they often became friendships that could be maintained over the years in the presence of new romances, giving life a continuity that the noncelibate romances didn't have. Had her only associations with men been romances, her relationships with the male world would have become a series of little unconnected byways. The discipline of her mind in not fantasizing sex with friends is what gave Tamiko the freedom to continue these friendships and to be friends with married men.

However, at twenty-nine, Tamiko took stock of her life. Fantastic friendships, a great career beginning, exciting service projects, good relationship with the church and God—but no marriage. She believed that if she honored God in remaining celibate, he would provide a husband for her, but as yet he had not. Was celibacy and friendship really the way to go? As she looked honestly at the women in her church singles' group, she acknowledged that the women who dated the most, who even seemed to be the most desirable as friends, were the divorced who were not prudish about sex. They were going to get their second turn before she had her first chance at marriage.

In honesty, Tamiko had to admit that she could have been married. It had been her choice to break the relationship with Larry—and it was not because of sex. She also had no misgivings about her decision, no longings when she saw Larry with his wife and new baby. Tamiko could not think of any friend whose husband she wanted. She had subconsciously chosen singleness up to this point in her life, but now was it too late to compete for marriage with nonvirgins? Virginity was not a premium quality at twenty-nine, Tamiko had discovered. She still rankled at the comment her last date had made when she maneuvered out of his embrace: "Who wants a thirty-year-old virgin? What are you saving yourself for?" More and more of the men she dated were divorced.

They also seemed to have more appeal than those never married. Why?

The men who had been married seemed to have a better idea of how to share feelings comfortably with a woman, Tamiko observed. Those never married seemed to be aloof, or to play sexist games—such as flattery, the kind of body-related comments that make a woman feel like an object rather than a person. Or the long-term single men in her life seemed to be so focused on ideas or projects that play and lightness disappeared. Perhaps, she thought, it was just that she was more uptight with those never married because she considered them more eligible.

Tamiko realized that she had not allowed her body to be aroused by a man since high school. Somehow, after the break with her high school boyfriend, she had not wanted her body aroused again without fulfillment. Now she wondered if her body would respond after the dormancy of the past ten years. Of course, she remembered, there were the times when a book or movie had aroused her and she had masturbated to release the body tension. So the body did still work, she mused. She had developed the habit, however, of using her mind and her time to keep busy with people and projects, so she was seldom aware of what she was missing. The fear of being left out only crept in at times like tonight, she thought, by letting what that rotten date had said about virgins undermine her convictions.

And that was it. What he had said bothered her only because she allowed it to. It was no more true now than in years past.

"Stop it, Tamiko," she told herself. "You have a good life. You'd rather be single than married to anyone who's available. So get busy, enjoy yourself, and stop moping around!" She laughed at herself, picked up the phone, and called a friend to go to a movie.

Tamiko's Beliefs and Their Results

Tamiko believed that men and women are more alike than different; therefore, she could have genuine friendships with men without playing games about romance or physical sex.

She had committed herself to keeping her mind free from any thoughts of sexual involvement with a man belonging to someone else. She believed that God would provide a husband for her in his time, if she remained celibate.

Tamiko was free to love both men and women genuinely in mutual friendships because of her freedom from seeing men as sex objects or women as competitors. She also escaped the confusion and heartache experienced by her friends whose principal contact with the opposite sex was romantic. Her lack of experience with sex and her strong feelings about being celibate, however, probably kept her from being as relaxed with "eligible" men as she was with male friends with whom the sex issue was settled in her mind.

Unfortunately, her belief that God gives every good person a spouse was not based on reality—God never promised a spouse for every one of his children. His intent for us is much larger than mating (although for most his plan is a mate). This error led Tamiko into serious conflict with God later in life.

Sex and Celibacy Are Habits

The divorced or widowed single whose body is accustomed to sex has a more difficult time being celibate than does the virgin or the person who has been an abstainer for several years. Our bodies are habitual creatures, getting used to meals at certain times and sex at certain times. For the first few months of separation, when the usual time for sex rolls around, the body gets prepared; and when nothing occurs, the person tends to feel the body's urgency.

The encouraging word, however, is that each month of abstention decreases the body's sexual demands, and also establishes a new habit of the body, celibacy. The habit of sex, of course, is much stronger and can be revived immediately because of the intense pleasure that sex can give. But the habit of celibacy can give freedom for pursuits other than sex.

Since most pastors are married and find it difficult to imagine being celibate themselves, it is sometimes difficult for them in a counseling situation to insist on the celibacy of their single parishioners. They are, appropriately, in the

33

habit of sex, so the strain of celibacy—even for a two-week conference away from their spouses—looms large. What they may not realize is that the habit of celibacy makes it easier for us.

Let us remember, that since sex is in the mind, the habits of the body are overruled by the mind's habits. A celibate mind is what gives real freedom.

Sex Has Wide Variations of Meaning

Unlike the need for water, food, and other physiological needs that must be fulfilled to live, the sex drive can permanently be unfulfilled and the abstainer can still live in health. Because of its power, yet lack of necessity, humans are free to invest sex with a much wider variety of meanings than we invest in eating or itching. Therefore, we each experience sex differently.

At the end of a first date, the differences in meaning that sex has for different persons become apparent. For example:

—A woman thinks, "He attacked me in the car. All he wanted was my body." Meanwhile the man thinks, "She's not responding to my kisses. She doesn't like me."

—Another woman says, "I guess I wasn't attractive to him; he didn't even ask to come in." But the man says, "I respected her too much to try anything on the first date."

—A divorcée exults, "He slept with me. Now he will be coming back." The man sighs, "She slept with me. I guess she's not worth seeing again."

—Another woman worries, "I went to bed with him. Now I'm no good." The bachelor worries, "Now that we've had sex she's going to make all kinds of demands on me."

Some people experience great guilt in having sex outside of marriage, but others feel none. Some find their masculinity or femininity at stake, while others are unconcerned. Those with great expectations of love often find disappointment in casual sex. The specific meaning of sex varies from person to person depending on one's expectations and assumptions. Usually, we are not aware of what sex means to us until we examine our own affirmative and negative responses to it or our feelings of sadness, envy, joy, or judgment about the affairs of others. Nor are we aware that its meaning is probably different for those whom we may choose as partners. Hence, there is great potential for hurt and disappointment or for hurting and disappointing others. This freedom to interpret sex also allows it to be used as a substitute for other needs or a symbol of other wants.

---

1. Find examples of responses to the same sexually arousing sight or situation that contrast because the mindset is different.

2. How would you interpret the intentions of a date who wants sex the first time you go out?

3. What are some meanings that sex can have for a person?

HOW SINGLES VIEW SEX

What singles do about sex can be divided into three general categories: (1) nonrelational or casual sex—looking at the physical experience as valid for one's own pleasure or need without necessarily building a caring relationship with the partner; (2) relational sex—that is, viewing the physical act as an extension of a caring, loving relationship; or (3) celibacy—choosing to abstain from sexual intercourse when single.

Nonrelational or Casual Sex

By *nonrelational sex* (often called casual sex) I do not mean sex without another person, but sex without a personal relationship or caring for the other person. I have divided this section on nonrelational sex into two categories: "sex as a fix" and "sex for fun." Although all of the classifications I have described actually overlap, even relational and nonrelational sex, separating types of motivation does help us to uncover belief systems and to observe consequences.

Sex As a Fix

Overuse of drugs, alcohol, and food have been acknowledged as escapes from reality, but sex? I ran across the concept of sex as a fix while interviewing a man who was associated with Alcoholics Anonymous. He said: "All men that are going from woman to woman are going to each for a

36

fix. They want the same thing an alcoholic wants: 'Fix my hurt. Keep me from looking at my problems. Help me feel better.' The danger of using sex as a fix," he pointed out, "is that it keeps one from examining and dealing with the real problems."

Tom the Schoolboy

No one at school had seemed to notice Tom until after the summer he turned thirteen, when he had grown six inches and developed a good set of shoulders. Girls looked at him adoringly, giggled, wrote his name on their notebooks, and grabbed his comb out of his back pocket so he would chase them. He discovered that girls liked to be caught and held; the harder they struggled, the longer he got to hold them.

When a teacher gave Tom a hard time because he hadn't done his homework, he would find a girl to chase on the way home from school and hold her until he felt important again. He didn't need alcohol or drugs; girls were his fix. By the end of ninth grade, the holding had slipped into intercourse, and he was no longer content with less.

Tom didn't consider that he used the girls he slept with, since they were always willing and he treated them kindly. Part of what made him feel good about himself, what assuaged the hurts and built his ego, was that he could give a woman pleasure. He prided himself on being a good lover. However, he was careful to spread his charm widely, not wanting to become involved emotionally with any of them.

The necessity to continually find new partners to provide his weekly fix put a strain on Tom. The time and energy it took to seek and convince a girl to participate in his sex play meant that he had to miss more and more activities with his old friends. He also found it tiring to have to deal with the reactions of some girls after sex. Their expectations made anonymity increasingly important, prompting him to continually seek new places to meet girls.

Tom's Belief System

Tom believed that he was doing girls a favor by giving them a good experience with sex, which indicates that he

37

believed sexual technique to be a more important part of sex than personal caring. Tom found also that he himself could get a good feeling from sex and act as a more loving, giving person for awhile.

When Tom abstained from sex for longer than a week, he began feeling unmanly and lacking in confidence. He concluded that the virginal guys in his church group were undersexed and a virile man needed sex regularly. He feared that he might lose his virility if he abstained from sexual intercourse for long.

---

1. How did Tom use sex as a fix?
2. What parts of Tom's belief system do you agree with, disagree with, and why?
3. Why do people act more loving after a satisfying sex experience?
4. What characteristics would Tom be developing if he faced his problems instead of escaping through sex?

The Test of Love in Sex as a Fix

Whatever the cover of helpfulness or kindness, sex to satisfy one's own needs is simply using others. Therefore, sex as a fix does not pass the test of agape-love.

Sex for Fun

It's an after work get-together, a Sierra Club hike, a Parents Without Partners family outing, a church square dance, a Singles' Conference, a college extension class. It's a place where singles meet.

The eyes investigate the possibilities. Smiles are eager. The vibration of tension and excitement over the unknown ricochet through the atmosphere as pairs form and reform. Each single adopts his or her own mingling mode. There is anticipation: Whom will I meet? Where will it lead? What is expected of me? Will I find what I am looking for?

The secular "dance and drink" meeting places are often overtly sexual while religious and interest-centered groups are more covert, but the same overtones are still there for those who are looking. Although many who frequent these meeting places are trying to use sex to overcome some problem, some are just looking for fun. If it happens, great; if it doesn't, nothing is lost.

Frannie: Looking for Pleasure

Frannie had recently moved back to San Francisco after completing her B.S. degree in Oregon. She had had two affairs since her marriage had ended. She still had some hopes of marrying Roger, one of her professors, but he was still in Oregon and she had not seen him for three months.

All of her energy for the past several months had been focused on building her career. Now she was ready to play a little, meet some men, and feel physically alive again. After a year and a half of regular sex with Roger, her body was demanding satisfaction, her mind needed laughter, and Frannie was lonely. She did not want a relationship that would be emotionally demanding right now because her career required her energy. Just a little fun, she thought, a nice, pleasurable evening with no strings attached, some satisfaction with no responsibility. The business world demanded her assertiveness; she wanted to be reassured of her softness, femininity, and playfulness.

Interaction was loud and lively by the time Frannie arrived at Gill's, a "pick-up place" near her office building. Although she danced and chatted continually, it was not until she had checked the crowd out the third time that she responded to the approach of a young attorney. When he suggested that they go to his condominium, she accepted with delight. But sex with him turned out to be so impersonal that she was appalled. The experience was mere bodily satisfaction with no closeness or tenderness at all. She was more lonely than ever for Roger when she arrived home that evening.

In spite of the disappointment, Frannie tried another singles' place a month later when her body once more insisted that she had spent enough time focusing on her career. She agreed to go to dinner with a pleasant, friendly faced man she had been talking and dancing with for an hour. Leaving her car in the parking lot she climbed into his smart sports car, eager for dinner at Fisherman's Wharf, but he wanted to stop by his apartment on the way. Although she preferred to wait for him in the car, when he chided her for her fearfulness, she felt silly resisting, so she walked in with him. But once inside he began to pressure her for bed before dinner—and the increasing pressure brought out all Frannie's resistance. His cajoling and playfulness eventually turned to anger and cold assertiveness.

Frannie stalked out to find a taxi, chagrined that she had allowed herself to be parted from her car, but thankful that this not-so-pleasant man had turned out to be only sexually aggressive, not sick. There had been a few moments when she had thought he might use force.

Frannie's Beliefs and Their Results

Frannie believed that she could satisfy her body without becoming emotionally involved with another person. What harm can there be in sex between two consenting adults? was her premise. Since Frannie's playful self had been developed in association with sex during her two previous affairs, she did not know how to be playful without it ending in bed. By denying herself sex, she was also closing the outlet for her fun-loving self.

Casual sex intensified rather than remedied loneliness for Frannie. Orgasm without a personal relationship did not satisfy Frannie's wants. Since she did not like splitting herself—having her body in total intimacy, but her mind and affections not involved in the union—she began looking for meaningful relationships.

The Test of Love for Sex for Fun

The acknowledged motivation of sex for fun is to satisfy oneself. One gives enough kindness to get a good orgasm,

40

but there is no pretense of caring for the other person as an individual. By agreement, sex for fun is mutual using, not love.

Since the point of sex for fun is to stay uninvolved and satisfy the body without personally relating to the individual inside the body, and because sex engaged in for one's own pleasure, and not for a caring relationship, becomes boring, pleasure-seekers need a variety of partners and experiences in order to maintain their level of pleasure. Again, this is using people, which is contrary to agape-love; furthermore, it denies the God-intended "one flesh" bonding to which sexual intercourse contributes. Romans 1:24-32, Galatians 5:19, and other scriptures make it clear that such immorality is not only offensive to God but damaging to the person and society.

---

1. How does a person develop playfulness with the opposite sex without becoming sexually aroused?
2. Why was Frannie dissatisfied with casual sex whereas many people seem to be satisfied?
3. What risks are involved in sex with a comparative stranger?
4. Why do some people prefer sex with a stranger?

Relational Sex

Relational sex can extend from the loving people who sleep with each person they care about (claiming, "I only sleep with my friends") to the engaged couples who intend to marry soon. These singles believe that sex enhances a relationship and shows one's love for another. This group can be subdivided into two more categories: "overlapping lovers" (those who alternate sleeping with two or more in caring relationships) and "one at a time lovers" (those experiencing exclusive relationships). Harry's story exemplifies an exclusive relationship that became an overlapping situation.

41

Overlapping Lovers: Harry's Story

Harry had been quite content in his exclusive relationship with Joan for the first ten months, but now Joan was wanting and pushing for marriage. Although he and Joan had been great companions on sailing trips, Harry had not thought of her for a marriage partner, a home, children—for any life beyond sailing. He was intrigued by the thought of marriage—but not to Joan.

Since Joan was the sister of his best friend, Joan and Harry often double-dated with her brother and his wife. They were all part of a very companionable group of persons who sailed together regularly. Harry liked Joan, was very comfortable in the arrangement they had drifted into, and did not want to hurt her; but Joan did not excite him. Harry had never felt that wild falling-in-love that he wanted from his bride-to-be; and the more Harry thought of marriage, the less he wanted Joan. But he didn't want the trauma of facing Joan and her brother, since a breakup would affect the whole sailing group.

When Alicia came to work at the clinic where Harry practiced, all of his body chemistry ignited. He spent every moment with her that was possible without upsetting the status quo with Joan and the group. When he began sleeping with Alicia, he knew that he was risking great hurt to Joan. This troubled him because he felt disloyal, knowing that Joan counted on his fidelity, as he had with her. He had never needed to hide anything from Joan before and had enjoyed the freedom of an open relationship.

Each week he slept with Alicia whenever possible, and on weekends he continued his regular pattern with Joan although he was often withdrawn. Joan questioned him about his aloofness, demanding to know what was wrong. The more her persistence pushed him, the greater his frustration grew. This strain of being pulled between a long-term, affectionate relationship, with its comfortable life-style, and a new, exciting lover resulted in Harry's being touchy and often angry. He was anxious to feel settled, to be

42

free to be open again, and to have the serenity of loyalty to one person. He cared for Joan and did not want to hurt her, but he wanted to be with Alicia.

Joan settled the matter for him one morning by arriving on his doorstep and demanding to come in while Harry tried to block the door because Alicia was in his bed. Rather than let Joan in to confront Alicia, Harry thought a minute and then stammered out the truth.

Harry's Beliefs and Their Results

Harry believed that sleeping with a person he was dating regularly caused far less tension than trying to be celibate. He expected fidelity in a sex relationship from himself as well as his partner, but he did not believe a commitment to marriage was necessary for sleeping together.

Although Harry was distressed that his friendship with Joan ended so harshly, he was relieved to be out of that fragmenting situation because he had suffered great tension during the overlap of lovers. Had he and Joan been friends rather than lovers during those good times of sailing, he might have kept Joan's and her brother's friendship, but the result of Harry's treatment of Joan also caused a split between Harry and his best friend.

Special Difficulties for Overlapping Lovers

Belonging and Exclusiveness

A woman's lover is angry with her because she isn't sleeping with anyone else. Although they have agreed that the relationship would not be exclusive, she has stated her right to sleep only with him if she chooses. He however is very uncomfortable, because he feels that her fidelity makes demands on him to be faithful also, even though she doesn't say so.

Most people make a tie between specialness and exclusiveness. Part of the desire for sexual union is the need we all have for belonging, to be most special to someone. If we give ourselves in sexual union tied to romantic love, most of us expect this to be a unique relationship in which we have top priority among this person's friends. That priority and loyalty, which the sexual relationship gives us, is what fills the need to be special. If we find that sex is not exclusive for the other partner, we no longer feel the specialness. For many men and women, it seems demeaning or produces anger to discover that one's lover is sleeping with someone else.

Comparisons

Many people feel uncomfortable if they fear they may be compared. In an exclusive relationship, people do not have to face the potential of rejection from mates who have found better lovers. Thus most people find that they are able to give and receive acceptance more freely with one lover than with several.

The Test of Love for Overlapping Relationships

The intent of overlapping sexual unions, even though love is involved, is to avoid permanent commitment. Therefore, as in nonrelational sex, the act is a lie; that is, the physical union is not directed toward becoming "one flesh"—which is the scriptural intent of sexual intercourse.

Furthermore, even though caring is felt in these relationships, they do not pass the test of love because loyalty is broken, hurt is almost certain, and loss of integration of the nonexclusive person almost always occurs. These are not indications of agape-love.

Conclusions About Nonexclusive Sex

Not many people can continue a life-style of overlapping lovers for long without beginning to separate body and emotions. To preserve their integrity, that is, their integration of love and sex, most who have experienced overlap move to the one-at-a-time phase of sexual activity. Thus, overlapping lovers is usually a temporary state, because if love increases, fidelity will increase, so the person will move to an exclusive relationship. If the overlapping pattern continues, caring emotions will increasingly need to be withheld, causing a separation of body and emotion, and therefore becoming a type of nonrelational act.

---

1. What causes the feeling of fragmentation among caring people who have overlapping lovers?
2. How does Scripture make clear that sleeping with more than one is not healthy?
3. Could Harry have had a continuing friendship with Joan if they had never had sex?

Singles As Exclusive, or One-at-a-Time Lovers

Although many singles go through times of confusion or hurt using sex as a fix, and some experience times of experimenting with sex, most people find one partner to be a more satisfying way of life. Those who are hooked on the glorious feeling of falling in love often move from partner to partner trying to recapture that feeling when the early symptoms of eros fade. Some move on rapidly because they have not developed any of the skills that are necessary to keep love alive, but many continue with the same lover over a long period of time, often into marriage.

The Test of Love for One-at-a-Time Relationships

The Committed Relationship

The area of relational sex that is the most difficult to assess on the principle of agape-love is the committed relationship prior to marriage. It feels like love; it looks like love; but does it pass the test of love? The considerations listed below,

45

which may help determine if a relationship is truly characterized by agape, apply to those intent on marriage as well as to those who play the one-at-a-time game from one to one to one.

Agape-love is responsible. The test of love requires that we consider the possible consequences to ourselves, to each other, to anyone else in our realm of responsibility, and to God.

If pregnancy is a possibility, agape involves deciding how both persons would give the child its best opportunity, how pregnancy would affect both partners, their families, friends, and their Christian community. Agape means taking responsibility for the possibility of a child by mutually deciding beforehand how pregnancy would be handled. If a man or woman is not willing to discuss and make a decision about pregnancy, then the relationship has not passed the test of love for each other or for the unborn child.

If either partner has children, agape insists that they be considered. In our schools today, many children come from households that include Mom's boyfriend or Dad's girl-friend. These children have to establish relationships with these multiple parental figures. Sometimes we think that older children are not affected, but if they are at an age of deciding their own roles, the parental role model can have a significant influence. If this hasn't been thoroughly dis-cussed and honest decisions made, the relationship has not passed the test of love.

Agape-love is responsible for preventing hurt to the partner where possible. Of course, we know that life gives no guarantees against hurt; people who abstain from sex also hurt each other, and married people often hurt their partners. However, we are responsible for examining our motivations and our knowledge of the other person to determine if we are deliberately heading for hurt.

Often one partner does not intend marriage and knows that the other expects or hopes the relationship will lead to marriage. To enter into an unequal sexual union such as this is irresponsible. The one desiring marriage is attempting to manipulate, hoping to change the other's mind, while the one not desiring marriage is using the other, knowing that his or her opposite objectives will be hurtful.

If there have been no conversations and decisions about the future together, about marriage, wants, dreams, family, and money—the when, where, and how of a married life together—then sexual union is a bodily function and does not pass the test of love.

Helping the Divorced

Some singles find themselves wanting to be a healing agent to the hurting divorced person. Often the reassurance the divorced most want and seem to need is a successful experience in bed. Does this pass the test of love? Many divorced are looking for someone to lean on, a relationship rather than a onetime fling in bed, so if the sexual relationship does not continue, two problems may occur. First, the ending may be interpreted by the hurting one as one more rejection. Second, if the divorced person is using the partner only to prove himself or herself or as a fix, this is using and not loving. Even impromptu "sex therapists" have feelings, so the hurting one is responsible to consider what this experience will do to the helping partner, since sex affects both persons.

On the other hand, if the relationship does last, it was begun too soon, while the divorced one was not yet healed. According to Jim Smoke, who has run divorce recovery seminars for many years, it takes one to two years for the divorced to become whole enough to be able to enter freely into a new relationship. People leaping immediately into new relationships are fragments looking for someone to fix life for them. They need time and space for individual development before adapting once more to marriage.

Responsible love might find better ways to give healing and wholeness to people who are hurting. Friendship would be much more valuable than sex at this point in a person's life.

47

Helping the Virgin

What about the older virgin who wants to experience sex? Is the test of love passed by the man or woman who offers help? (The virgin is certainly not thinking of the spiritual growth of the helper, since his or her obvious using does not pass the test of love.) Sex without love and commitment is only a physical experience. If the single acting as "sex therapist" does initiate the virgin, it would be to the shell of the experience only, to knowledge of the body without the soul and spirit. What then? Does the sexual bond become an emotional bond for one partner? For both? Does this open the door for desire so that the former virgin's body makes demands it did not make before, keeping him or her from pursuing more meaningful relationships or developing and using his or her gifts?

One woman who was almost forty before experiencing sex became obsessed with finding good sex. The "shell" experience did not satisfy her, but by centering her search on physical fulfillment rather than on loving relationships, she was in a continually empty circle. Another common experience is to fall in love with the sex initiator, which often results in years of one-sided love.

All of these tests of love for one-at-a-time sexual liaisons indicate that it is rarely agape-love—responsible, caring love—that prompts sex outside of marriage. Almost always it is the demands of the body or incorrect knowledge, which overcome the faint protest of the mind and spirit.

Adultery

Sleeping with someone else's spouse obviously does not pass the test of love for the spouse and children involved, or for oneself, which many discover through their pain. But there is another test of Scripture to be considered. God takes vows very seriously, as indicated in Numbers 30:2; "When a man vows a vow to the Lord, . . . he shall not break his word; he shall do according to all that proceeds out of his mouth." So to participate in someone's breaking of a vow is not

48

showing love of God. We get caught up in adultery very easily by saying, "He's separated." "She says her marriage is already dead." "Everyone divorces these days." But a person's word, one's promise or vow, is very important to God. God's word created the world; our salvation depends on his promise. To be like God, our word must be sure, and we must respect the vows of others.

So even if we think that the spouse does not care, there are no children to consider, and there have been others before us, love for God would prevent us from participating in the breaking of a vow.

The Spiritual Bond

The scriptural interpretation of Paul in 1 Corinthians 6:12-20 would prohibit sexual intercourse from all but those committed to marriage, since sexual intercourse creates physical and emotional elements of the "one flesh" bond. For the committed, the question remains, Is the act a lie? Is the spiritual one flesh intended by the physical union of two bodies a reality before marriage, or is there a holding back, a hesitancy, that allows some deceit in the act? Paul's statement in 1 Corinthians 6:12 tells us that an act may be lawful—at least not against a specific law—but is the act helpful? Does sexual intercourse before marriage in any way acknowledge the enslavement of the body to its own desires? Does it demean the body as the temple of the Holy Spirit? These, I believe, are questions for each individual couple to handle.

---

1. Should Christian women use birth control?
2. Is abortion an acceptable way for a Christian single to deal with pregnancy?
3. At what point should pregnancy be discussed in a dating relationship?
4. Could it ever be God's best plan for an engaged couple to have sexual intercourse? Why?

Celibacy

People who know how to love and understand the value of celibacy will probably remain celibate until marriage, or permanently if marriage does not occur. Those whose belief systems waver may move into sex for fun in an isolated situation (such as a vacation) or as an experimental risk, not staying long in this category if they are truly healthy and know how to love. Or in a true love relationship they may risk a total sexual relationship before marriage. If the relationship fails, the most healthy will probably return to celibacy.

The healthy celibate is one who has learned to love both sexes without sexual intercourse. Those married are also commanded to love both sexes celibately, with the exception of one person, the spouse. Whether one is male or female, the goal is the same: love your neighbor—both sexes, all ages, everyone—as yourself, with concern, interest, and enjoyment.

Jonathan the Purposeful

Jonathan did not believe his friends when they quoted, "If you don't use it, you lose it." He was determined to have sex with his as yet unknown, future wife only. He was fortunate to have had female cousins, so he had grown up knowing girls as friends. Both sports and knowing girls as real persons during high school helped him to develop a discipline during his teens that carried him through his twenties. Working with girls in his Inter-Varsity chapter during college strengthened his respect for women as friends to care for. Over his five years in college, he had seriously thought of several women as possible marriage partners, but he wanted to settle in one place before he started a family.

Jon's parents had been married at nineteen as virgins and had never been unfaithful to one another. Their obvious love for each other and enjoyment of the marriage bed gave him confidence to ignore the urgings of his friends who said that he needed experience to be a good lover. Jon's mother had confided to him once that even though sometimes she was tempted to say that she was too tired when his father approached her, she would recall the tender closeness always present afterward and her tiredness would melt. Jon had been able to see past his mother's overweight body and the sagging chinline to the shy smile as his mother confessed that she felt beautiful and cherished in bed with his father. His father had made sex a giving, binding union, unique, with no comparisons. Jonathan wanted to be that kind of a lover. Practice with other women would defeat, not enhance, that objective.

Jon played semi-pro baseball, then moved on to a career with the F.B.I. Something strong and protective about Jonathan drew women to him, but he had no intention of giving himself to anyone but the woman he chose to marry. He held out until he found her at age thirty-one. From his wife's quiet glow and his pleased glance when friends mentioned marriage intimacies, it appeared that both were glad he had been celibate while single.

---

1. How would you answer the fear "If you don't use it, you lose it"?
2. Do people need experience in lovemaking before marriage?
3. How can a man be healthy, manly, and celibate all through his teens, twenties, and thirties?
4. What are the advantages and disadvantages of waiting for sex until marriage?

Sally the Temporary Celibate

After the shock of the divorce and her ex's remarriage, Sally began dating to restore her wounded ego. However,

51

finding herself restless with the constant searching and parrying, she decided to use her time in a more satisfying manner. Turning to the church, she became part of a lay counseling program in her church and joined the visitation team. Working with these dedicated people was exciting, but it suddenly occurred to her that she was now an example—looked on as a leader in her church. Although she had not particularly planned on being celibate—after all, she was not a virgin and her body had its needs—she decided to commit herself to celibate dating for the duration of her commitment to the lay counseling program. Since she had just ended a not-too-exciting dating relationship, the decision was not too difficult. Sally could not imagine committing herself to permanent celibacy, yet she was not keen on the idea of remarrying. As a single, she had too many paths in life to explore yet.

At first she felt awkward in saying no to her dates—after all, her son was in college, she was living alone, who was to care? She almost broke her self-imposed standard with one personable man, since no one had demanded the commitment of her and she felt as if perhaps she was just punishing herself. But two years—the amount of time she had committed to the counseling center—wasn't impossible, she reasoned, and it certainly couldn't hurt her.

By the end of the first year, she found that her relationships with men were different; they were friends now, rather than "dates." As friends, she found herself caring for their lives. She and a man from her visitation team met for a bite to eat before each team meeting. Since their friendship had originated in a ministry, they had never played the using roles with each other that are typical of dating. Although this man was a regular in her life, there was no ownership, and she felt free to have other male friends also. The desire for sex with any of her male friends was simply not part of her thinking. When her body urged her to think about sex, she could not imagine a situation in which it could seem appropriate or desirable with any of the men she knew, nor did she desire it with a stranger. The first year of celibacy had made the second year seem easy.

Sally loved her freedom of time in the mornings. With no one to cook for or to distract her, she could rise early and take her coffee to her favorite contemplation spot, curling up with her Bible. She loved singing aloud to the Lord without the embarrassment of someone hearing.

Coming home after work in the evening, Sally would sometimes feel guilty about her delight in having her unwinding time to herself. No dinner to cook, no egos to mend, no chatter to listen to. What joy to be in charge of her own time—the freedom to call whom she chose, to be with a variety of persons of her choice. Right after her divorce Sally had not realized the necessity of scheduling people into her life, since she had been used to having someone in the house all the time. But once she realized that people were not going to drop in and that it was up to her to plan "people" time, she found her own people-rhythm: four nights with people and three alone. Sally had found that she was more contemplative than some of her friends, who needed five or six evenings with people, and she loved the freedom to arrange her schedule according to her best functioning.

After two years of celibacy, Sally found that she was more caring in her relationships with men. She was free to be friends without expecting them to perform according to a defined role. As she walked across the church patio on a Sunday morning, she would find herself stopped by men and women of all ages wanting to talk with her on a wide variety of subjects. At work, also, she felt affirmed by the response to her work and relationships.

Sally's Beliefs and Their Results

Sally felt that singles in leadership should be celibate and that she could maintain celibacy for a limited amount of time. She wondered if it was right to find living alone so enjoyable.

Sally's body became used to celibacy and its demands for sex decreased to the point that when she considered the whole of herself, she didn't want sex without the fully committed relationship. When her body wanted sex, all she needed to do was to consider the act in any real situation that she could imagine, and then she would know that her body wasn't speaking for the whole of her.

By focusing on relationships within her interests, rather than on dates from social situations, she found much more depth in her friendships with men than she had in her previous dating. Pursuing her interests, using her gifts for ministry, and recognizing the contemplative part of herself that loved to spend time alone and with God, provided for her a richer life than frantically dating or worrying about sex.

---

1. How do you feel about Sally's belief that singles in church leadership should be celibate?

2. At what points in one's life is it easiest to make a commitment to celibacy? How was Sally's timing appropriate?

3. What makes people who enjoy being alone, as Sally did, feel guilty? Is it legitimate to enjoy living alone, or does God intend for us to live in families or communities?

4. If Sally had not kept her commitment to celibacy, how do you think she might have handled the lapse? Is it appropriate to make short-term commitments of this kind?

===============3===============

EFFECTS OF SEX AMONG SINGLES

========================= S ome truths about sex that have not been explored adequately by either the secular or the religious worlds, yet seem to apply consistently to singles experiencing sex, are: its bonding effect, its splitting effect, and its fragmenting effect. Sex also seems to inhibit emotional growth in those who use it as a substitute for other wants or needs, and it interferes with intimacy outside of a totally committed relationship.

The Bonding Effect

The intent of sex, as indicated in Genesis 2:24, is to help make two persons one flesh. As persons experience the intensity of physical intimacy for the first time, a feeling of love and tenderness for the partner usually arises, even if this person was only a casual date an hour earlier. The assumption that there is a bond finds support in a number of ways in the dating world. If a woman finds a likely candidate for a long-term relationship whom she doesn't want to lose, she may expect that sex will ensure a longer time of exploration. Men, too, often want to pin down a prospect— that is, be able to count on loyalty—by sex. The fact that sex always changes a relationship between two persons supports the idea of the bonding effect of sex.

Steve the Proper

Marcia, his pastor's niece, was a virgin when Steve met her, but Steve had had sex relations with his two previous girlfriends. The pastor had given Marcia a big buildup, and Steve knew that the pastor thought it was time for Steve to marry since he was twenty-three and had a steady job. Steve was prepared to seriously consider Marcia, and the phone conversation they had before he saw her intrigued him even more. He was disappointed however when he first saw her, since physically she just wasn't his type. Although her personality was appealing, Steve might not have dated her again if it hadn't been for his feeling of obligation to his pastor. He was surprised at Marcia's response to him sexually since the pastor had emphasized her spiritual qualities. He had made the usual advances but had expected Marcia to resist. Because of the pastor he tried to hold back, but the habit of sex overruled his thoughts. If she hadn't been a virgin, or if she hadn't been the pastor's niece, he might have wiggled out of the situation. But actually she fit everything on his checklist except some silly image of the physical ideal he had in his head that he felt should not be important.

Steve could think of no valid reason not to marry Marcia. Both families favored the match, their friends at church thought it was ideal, and the pastor was eager for them to set the date. Steve could not find any excuse to delay, so they walked down the aisle.

Steve was reasonably content, although often irritable when with her alone, until she wanted to get pregnant. Then he realized with full force that he did not want her to bear his child. He did not want to be married to her—he never had. He felt pressured and trapped.

Marcia's Beliefs

Marcia felt from the night she met Steve that he was everything she wanted, but sensed that the feeling was not mutual. She felt that sex might trap him into marrying her, risking that Steve would not back out once they had had sex.

Steve's Beliefs

Steve believed that sex before engagement was wrong, especially with someone from the church, so his guilt interfered with his judgment. Since he believed that he should get married, he was vulnerable to the advice of people he respected, and he trusted his pastor's and family's judgment more than his own.

The Results of Steve's and Marcia's Beliefs

The bonding effect of sex before a clear decision to marry had been made clouded important issues and feelings for both Steve and Marcia. Steve's guilt kept him from listening to his own inner self, which had been telling him all along that this was not the woman he wanted to love the rest of his life. Marcia demeaned herself by trying to trap Steve, rather than regarding herself of equal worth. She risked tremendous rejection because of her manipulation.

---

1. How might Steve's and Marcia's relationship have been different if they had delayed sex?
2. What alternatives do they have at this point in their marriage?
3. Was the pastor acting appropriately in introducing them and encouraging marriage?
4. How can we be most helpful in giving advice to others?

Kate: Not Available for Marriage

Unfortunately, the emotional bonding of a sexual relationship cannot be turned off at will; it must run its course. Kate had drifted away from God and the church because the singles' crowd she had become a part of usually went sailing on Sundays. Although she believed that she would never marry someone who wasn't a Christian, she became sexually involved with Sonny, who would have nothing to do with

God or the church. It was her first physical experience and eros was exceedingly strong. Sonny sensed her ambivalence and each periodically pulled away from the relationship, but then one or the other would reach out and they would merge again with renewed intensity.

During one separation, when Kate was on vacation, she ran into Henry, an old friend from her church group whom she had always admired and had once hoped to marry. They began corresponding when her vacation was over. Her relationship with Sonny continued to ebb and flow although the intensity was diminishing, and Kate really wanted to be emotionally free. When Henry was temporarily transferred to an office in Kate's city, Kate found the strength to leave Sonny completely. Gradually Kate's and Henry's relationship progressed to engagement.

When Henry was transferred back to his home office, he and Kate set the wedding date. Kate was delighted to be marrying someone from her own background, someone whose values and life-style she respected, someone whose children she wanted to bear. But when Henry left, Sonny came back into Kate's life. She wanted to resist him, but the habit of the familiar overpowered her. The little doubts and hesitations she had about marriage and Henry were magnified. Guilt overwhelmed her; she knew that Henry would be devastated if he discovered what she had done.

She broke the engagement feeling that she could not yet give herself completely to Henry. She needed more healing time.

Kate had known, even when she broke her engagement to Henry, that she would never marry Sonny, but she found solace with him after the breakup with Henry because Sonny was familiar and comfortable. It took another year of on-again–off-again before Kate made the final break with Sonny. She longed then to get in touch with Henry, realizing the quality of person and life that she had given up, but by then she was embarrassed and ashamed to call. Finally risking a phone call, she discovered that Henry was married. The tone of his voice told Kate that his feeling for her was not dead, but it was too late.

Kate's Beliefs and Their Results

Kate believed that ignoring church would not affect her Christian life or her chances for a Christian marriage. Having no idea of the emotional power of sex, she believed that she could walk out of a sex relationship any time she wanted to, and that she could marry by the effort of her will even though her emotions were not free. All of these beliefs were erroneous.

Being uninvolved in the church and totally involved socially with sexually active singles made her vulnerable to an affair. The power of sexual intercourse bound her emotionally when she wanted to be free to marry someone appropriate, nor did she give Sonny a clear view of Christianity.

---

1. How does Kate's experience demonstrate the "one flesh" concept of Scripture?
2. What pulled Kate back to Sonny, when rationally and deliberately, she had chosen Henry?
3. Is there anything friends from the church could have done if Kate had returned to church before she broke the engagement?

Larry the Serviceman

Another case of unwanted bonding occurred when an airman had wanted a temporary relief from loneliness. In only three months Larry's tour of duty would be over, he explained to the chaplain, and he didn't know what to do. "The woman I've been seeing is pregnant and wants me to marry her and take her to America."

Larry had been only eighteen when he arrived in Korea. At the remote Air Force base where he was stationed, the only American women he ever saw were two missionaries who came to the base chapel occasionally. He had been a faithful Christian in his home church, but loneliness had become almost a sickness during his first few months in this isolation. One of his barracks mates had encouraged him to go to a local dance hall where he could meet a Korean girl. Several weekends later he took Ocho to an apartment several guys had rented off base.

Larry had been with Ocho regularly for the past year, even though at first she knew almost no English. She had been as innocent as he when they started their sex life together. Ocho had treated him well, but he had thought of these eighteen months as a hiatus in his life, not real—not meaningful to his future.

What would he do? Ocho would not fit in his hometown. He had expected to go back and enjoy bachelorhood in America for awhile. He was not ready to be married and a father.

Ocho had told him that because she had disgraced the family by living with a man, she would not be accepted in her father's or brother's homes. Korean women do not live alone, so her only alternatives if he didn't marry her were to find another serviceman to take care of her or to become a prostitute. Being pregnant might make either of these prospects difficult.

His child would have very little chance, the chaplain told him. Most servicemen's children were abandoned by school age because they were not accepted in Korean society. As street children they had to steal to live and almost inevitably ended up in jail.

Larry's Beliefs and Their Results

Larry knew that sex with this Korean woman was wrong, but he believed that his loneliness, and the fact that the girl offered herself, justified the situation. He believed in loyalty, responsibility, and love, which made the decision far more difficult for him than for other, more self-centered, servicemen. He had allowed himself to compartmentalize his life, thinking that what happened so far away from home would not affect the rest of his life.

Larry cannot maintain both the style of life he desires in the next few years and his sense of responsibility. His year with Ocho will permanently affect him, even if he leaves her, as will his knowledge of being a father.

---

1. What do you think Larry will do and why?
2. How else might Larry have handled his loneliness?
3. In what ways do people compartmentalize their lives in order to justify sex?

Undesirable Bonding

In each of the above cases, sex created a bond that was unexpected. The bonding became bondage when the people involved needed to be free, but couldn't. Emotional bonding to a person who is desirable for the moment but undesirable as a life partner may occur when people are unaware of the bonding effect of sex, leaving the man or woman feeling morally bound to marry someone unsuitable. On the other hand, a person may not be emotionally free to marry someone who is suitable because of entanglements that have not been healed. Then, intense disappointment messes up the lives of these disillusioned lovers, who would have been less vulnerable had they not sealed their love with physical bonding.

We have all known of single women spending years of their lives waiting for their lovers to divorce. Most of us know of couples of different religions unable to give their children any religious teaching, such as the Moslem and Christian who are bringing up their children with no religion. American college women may find international students exotic on campus, but living in their countries, with their families and customs, can require tremendous adjustment. Servicemen are faced with the dilemma of what to do about their half-American children, or the women they have learned to love but who would not fit into their home culture. Some people who have accidentally become bonded do marry and overcome the intense differences, but many go their separate ways with a feeling of great loss.

The bonding, which is tremendously important in marriage, is often detrimental to the single, yet the alternative is to be split.

The Splitting Effect

George the Happy-go-lucky

George's first love affair was at the age of twelve when his sixteen-year-old neighbor seduced him. George was amazed at the feelings of tenderness and love he felt as he experienced this intimacy, although he had viewed her as just an ordinary teenager a few hours earlier. He plotted every way to be with her until, discovering that she had a boyfriend with whom she slept also, George became violently jealous. To get even, he found another girl to make love to, but he wasn't about to let himself love the new girl. He used her to get over his attachment to his first love. George had begun the separation of body and emotion.

After his first experience, George held back his feelings of love, but now that his body had experienced the pleasure of intercourse, he sought opportunities to satisfy it. He enjoyed the conquest and the feeling of masculinity that these experiences gave him.

He had learned to quell any spontaneous declarations of caring, even when the delight of union brought such thoughts to his lips. He practiced focusing his mind on the bodily sensations, separate from any caring for the person. Girls fell for him, but he did not want to be trapped by responsibility, or to be limited in seeking new experiences.

Four years in the service further ingrained the "love them and leave them" attitude in George. With the words of caring held back, he was increasingly aware of an emptiness in his relationships with women.

It was automatic for him to make the offer of sex to any attractive woman. After all, someone might question his masculinity if he didn't. He also recognized that women begin to question their attractiveness if men don't make the attempt, so kindness sometimes prompted the offer when he wasn't even interested.

Sometimes he was shocked at the affirmative responses. An older woman, whom he had kindly and jokingly propositioned while a group was having coffee after the singles' meeting, invited him to stop by her apartment after his racquetball game the following night.

When she opened the door wearing a beautiful negligee with candles, wine, and music in the background, obviously ready for her initiation into the sexually active life, he didn't know whether to laugh or run. After forty years as a virgin, she wanted to know how the rest of the world lived. Gallantly he "deflowered" her, much against his moral code, which said, "Never virgins, never married women, and never women from the church."

The division between sex and love was well established by age twenty-eight, when he began to think about marriage, but his experience was in choosing women who would keep it light and claim no responsibility from him. Wanting to be close to a woman, but finding no intimacy in his sexual experiences, George hoped that marriage would provide that sense of belonging that he lacked.

George began looking for attractive women with whom he could enjoy conversing, and who didn't submit to his pressure to get them into bed. He was frustrated if he wasn't successful with them, but on the other hand he was afraid of anyone too easy. He had slept with so many married women who had pursued *him* that it seemed impossible to find someone who would be faithful.

Mary Ann, who taught at a local college and was advancing rapidly toward administration as openings for women increased, resisted his sexual advances, but he found himself attracted enough to continue dating her. George enjoyed meeting people in new fields and found her stimulating.

It took two months of regular dating before he wore down her resistance to his sexual advances. Although sex with Mary Ann did not set any bells ringing, he felt a responsibility since he had spent all this time winning and reassuring her.

He used all of his techniques to help her enjoy sex, but he could not feel any emotions of love in the sex act himself. Tender words did not feel appropriate, so he demonstrated his choice of her by gifts and admiration of her career, but she longed for tender words whispered in her ear. However, since George and Mary Ann were both thirty-two, tired of the singles' circuit, and ready for a home, marriage seemed the next appropriate step.

George found faithfulness to Mary Ann very difficult since he was used to variety and spontaneity. When Mary Ann became pregnant, she moved into a separate bedroom—not what George's anticipation of marriage had been, and his business trips became more frequent.

George recognized that in marriage, sexual intimacy depends on the total relationship, but he could not connect verbal intimacy with bodily sex. He didn't expect Mary Ann to be as cooperative sexually as his pickups were, but the habit of easy gratification was strong. In his mind, the quick sex-for-fun affairs he had on business trips were not being unfaithful since no emotion was involved, no meaning, just bodily satisfaction.

George's Beliefs and Their Results

George saw no harm in sex between consenting adults. Sex was natural and enjoyable, and therefore to be enjoyed like good food or good wine. George believed that adultery (taking another person's spouse) and deflowering virgins were wrong. Sex with a pickup for whom he had no feeling he did not consider adultery. However, for George, a greater wrong than adultery or deflowering was the wrong of hurting someone's feelings.

The separation of sex and love was clear-cut in George because of the many years of practice he had had. At first the physical union had brought with it a sense of oneness with the person, and words of caring popped out. But he learned to stifle those spontaneous utterances since they were inappropriate when the coupling was over. He learned to hold back feelings until he didn't even know if he had the capacity to love. He could identify the feeling of conquest, but when the conquest was over all feeling left him.

He lacked trust in women because of his experiences, possibly causing him to choose a nonresponsive wife. However, the habit of easy gratification made his own faithfulness very difficult in marriage.

He never found the intimacy he desired and for several reasons. One, he had habitually hidden and squelched his feelings so that he didn't even know his emotions to be able to share them. Second, his early focus on sex kept him from developing friendship relationships with women, where he could learn to share his feelings. For him, women were sex objects (challenges to be conquered) rather than real persons. This lack of experience with women as persons may have limited his choice of a wife to someone who also had little experience in personal intimacy. Third, his life-style kept him from honesty, which is essential for intimacy.

The habits of adolescence had resulted for George in a diminished capacity for joy in marriage.

Explaining the Split

One effect of impersonal sex is always present—the internal split between sex and love, even though the split between body and emotions is imperceptible at first. A natural unity exists between our bodies and our emotions so that when the body is most intimate with another body, emotions of intimacy naturally surface. Usually the novice has a great desire to say, "I love you" and to express tenderness, loyalty, and a wish for continued unity.

However, if the partner was chosen for experimentation or gratification rather than for a committed relationship, these declarations of bonding are inappropriate. Loving words create opportunities for one partner to develop expectations

65

of a continuing relationship that the other may not want. Therefore, persons who want only casual sex quickly learn to quell these spontaneous declarations of caring. They learn to hold the emotions apart from the body, to practice focusing on physical sensations separate from any caring for the person.

Yet when the words of caring *are* spoken in the midst of passion, but seem totally inappropriate when the heartbeat slows, one is conscious of another kind of deceit. The words express one's own desire for integration of body and emotions at the moment of sexual union, but not a desire to continue caring for this specific individual. Therefore, this impulsive speaker experiences a loss of integrity both internally and externally. The passionate words have become a lie and an embarrassment if remembered by the momentary partner. Thus, most people find it more comfortable to hold back the words in order to experience only the internal loss of integration rather than deal with the expectations of another individual.

---

1. Why is it that even a secular man often does not want to deflower a virgin he is not in love with, even when he believes there is no harm in sex between consenting adults? What does this imply about the first experience of the sex act?

2. George's neighbor probably thought she was doing George a favor by initiating him into the sex act. How was this damaging rather than helpful?

3. How do both men and women get involved in sex by trying to be kind, or trying not to hurt someone's feelings? Is this true kindness?

4. What is the relationship between holding back feelings and the inability to experience personal intimacy?

The Fragmenting Effect

Frannie: Caring for Three Lovers

Frannie's dating experience as a young executive in San Francisco had left her thoroughly disgusted with the idea of sex for fun (as we saw in chapter 2). She had determined that any future sexual intimacy would come under circumstances of caring, or not at all. But now, five years after her divorce and fifteen months after attaining a management position in San Francisco, she had a problem: She cared deeply for three men, and could not reconcile the relationships.

When Clay, her ex-husband, had asked her for a divorce, her feeling had been one of utter hopelessness. She was twenty-five and had nothing: no role to play, no identity, no degree, no child, no career. There wasn't any hope for a good life. As a divorcée, what could she expect? Everything good had been ruined, according to all she had been taught. Even five years later a touch of loss—not for Clay but for the ideal—still stung her.

Her marriage had seemed perfect at first, exactly what she had always dreamed of; he was her dream image in looks, popularity, and money-making potential. They had been admired as an ideal couple at the Christian college where they had met. When Clay graduated and was immediately offered a position in a public relations firm, Frannie dropped out of college to marry him. Clay was her life. As they became active in the church where other Christians in Clay's firm attended, Frannie joined all the proper auxiliaries and became adept at entertaining for both business and church.

A sickening, leaden knot in her stomach pained her for days after she heard of Clay's first affair. Self-doubt assailed her: Where had she failed? What was wrong with her? What should she have done differently? She had done her best to please Clay in bed, although her body had never truly freed itself from the pattern of repression she had developed in that strained year before her marriage when she had struggled to maintain her virginity. Although her body did

67

not respond, she pretended orgasms and Clay didn't seem to know the difference.

Her fear of divorce was so intense that it aggravated all the weaknesses of the marriage, until Clay's withdrawal and her grasping made life together unbearable. Against his command, she even stopped taking birth control pills, hoping that a child would cement the marriage or at least give her some sense of worth in life.

She had done everything she thought God required of her and it had not worked.

After the divorce Frannie moved to San Francisco, where she began her life over, feeling she was a failure and needing to know who she was and who she could be. At that point Tom (whom we met in chapter 2) entered the picture. He was a forty-five-year-old bachelor, and had learned the art of listening while traveling to major cities in the West and Midwest as a company representative. A longtime family friend, he had heard of her move to California, and while in town on business he called and she invited him over for the evening.

Frannie poured out her feelings and fears to Tom, for the first time admitting her failure to have an orgasm, blaming herself and her sexual inadequacy for the divorce. Tom was very tender as he assured her that he had serious doubts about her frigidity, that he suspected that Clay's selfishness and clumsiness had caused her lack of response. He wondered aloud if he could help heal some of her emotional trauma by proving to her that she wasn't frigid.

(Looking back, Frannie could smile knowingly as she remembered Tom's approach, knowing him much better now and having experienced more men than in her newly divorced innocence. But since Tom had helped her self-esteem immeasurably, she still appreciated him.)

Tom moved very slowly with Frannie, listening, assuring, laughing, advising. He sat on the side of her bed, holding her while she sobbed away some of the tension of failure, comforting her until she could sleep. For the first time in months—perhaps even years—Frannie felt worth. She suspected that this comfort was leading toward sex, which she had been taught was wrong, but everything she had been taught was questionable now. She had pleaded with God to save her marriage and he hadn't; what more did she have to lose? Even though Frannie had no great desire for sex, she was a pleaser. This man had given her hope, had made her begin to feel a person again, so she wanted to express her appreciation and would not risk putting him down. If that's what he wanted, that's what she would give.

It wasn't until their third night together that comfort flowed into arousal for Frannie. Unlike Clay, Tom had the discipline and sensitivity to focus on her needs so that in the next few nights Frannie found a new image of herself as a sexual being. She immediately began to think of marrying Tom, until he helped her to see their relationship as a growth experience for Frannie rather than a commitment. Later she realized that Tom hadn't been even faintly interested in committing himself to marriage; it was for that reason he had been so eager to help her focus on finishing her degree and beginning a career, on knowing herself before plunging into another marriage, and on experiencing men her own age rather than tying herself to a husband twenty years older.

Frannie was faithful to Tom for over a year after that initial week. Tom had managed a monthly visit at first, then slid back to his regular company schedule of two-month intervals, meeting Frannie in Portland when she moved to Eugene to finish college. By then Frannie had changed from her first intense grasping after marriage to an appreciation of Tom and of herself.

When she and Roger, a young professor, met at college, they formed a fun and caring relationship almost immediately. Frannie struggled inside over sex, wondering if she was the kind of woman who would go to bed with a third person—this time not even talking about marriage. Since she was not committed to Tom, she had no idealism or fear to keep her abstaining; yet since sex and caring were equated in her mind, it seemed natural to go to bed with Roger. Again she found herself with high expectation of marriage, but being wiser she didn't let her desire show with such grasping intensity as she had with Tom. However, as graduation approached, her anxiety grew. Since nothing in Eugene compared to the job offered her in San Francisco, it made no sense for her to stay in Eugene without a promise of marriage—but how she longed for Roger to want her!

Graduation day came and went. Roger was comfortable in his bachelorhood, so she reluctantly headed back to California.

Her brief excursion into casual sex during her first months after returning to San Francisco showed her that it wasn't for her. She wanted to keep body and emotions together, sleeping only with men whom she really cared about, but she didn't want to be committed to just one person. Her career had finally become more important than marriage, now that she had an identity of her own. Roger was still important to her, and Tom, of course, was a dear to whom she would always be obligated.

During the next year she dated a number of other men—men she cared about and enjoyed. On one occasion she found herself thinking, If I care as much about Jeff as I do about Roger, then why not express my caring in bed? Then, after a few dates with another delightful man, she reasoned, Since I like Ben as much as Jeff, how can I not sleep with him too? Because Frannie's body was accustomed to sex and she had no idealism left about the perfect marriage, the idea of abstinence did not seriously occur to her. She continued dating, and began to grow more and more attached to Jeff.

The day came when Tom came to San Francisco to stay, and she found that their relationship was not as comfortable as it had been. His position with the company was in question. Furthermore, Frannie sensed that at fifty Tom was not as successful with women as he had formerly been. He needed her to help him through this crisis. How could she say no to an old friend whose self-image was so shaky right now?

Tom moved in with her until he could find a house of his own. Then one morning, a few days later, while Frannie was preparing breakfast for the two of them, the phone rang. She grabbed it quickly, glad for the extension where Tom couldn't overhear her conversation.

It was Roger. "Hi, honey. I'm going to be in town this weekend!" Her stomach tightened. He went on to explain that he would be doing some work at San Francisco State and would be there for the full quarter. He would arrive Saturday night.

Frannie let her breath out with a whoosh as she hung up the phone. She kept very busy with toast, eggs, rescuing overdone bacon, and serving coffee for the next few minutes while she regained her composure. The first priority was to get Tom settled in an apartment. She had three days before Roger arrived.

She must get both Tom and Roger established in apartments not too close to hers so she could have some breathing space—and some time for Jeff, who had become more important to her than either of these earlier men in her life. The idea of pushing Tom out one door while Roger came in the other was appalling to her.

She had never mentioned her relationship with Tom to Roger or Roger to Tom. She suspected that they each had other lovers, but the subject was never mentioned. So much had to be hidden in this kind of living. Frannie sighed, thinking of the simpler life in Eugene with only Roger and a few clandestine trips to Portland.

Four weeks later, each was settled in his own apartment, and Frannie was not only continuing to see both but was also carrying on her usual life with Jeff. She felt fragmented. Constantly changing stained sheets seemed to be the symbol of her life.

The spontaneous, free giving that had started each of these relationships had faded as Frannie tried to give too much in too many directions. Trying to please, keep track of, empathize with, and personally relate to three lovers as a truly loving person—what Frannie wanted to do—had become a burden. In no way could each be most special, so Frannie found herself withdrawing from everyone. To continually share her personal self with these overlapping lovers became fragmenting. Therefore, to preserve her own wholeness as well as her spontaneity, she moved out of the situation.

71

Frannie's Beliefs and Their Results

Frannie believed that sex and love belonged together. If she loved someone and felt sexually attracted to him, she felt that sex was an appropriate way of showing love. Although Frannie believed adultery to be immoral and sex without love to be a misuse of her body, she could not see any harm in sex between loving, single adults.

But in the course of time she felt her life disintegrating. Frannie found it difficult to talk to one lover about another, and uncomfortable to talk to her friends about her lovers—especially about more than one. Since she couldn't be completely open, it became confusing to remember to whom she had told what, so she found herself screening her words very carefully or actually lying more and more.

Frannie was really worried about hurting Tom, nor did she want to hurt Roger or Jeff. She felt all three men had certain rights to her time and priorities, which became difficult to balance, especially since her new life with Jeff required increasing priority. The risk of losing Jeff because of Roger and Tom was creating tremendous tension for Frannie.

Frannie felt her loyalty, her caring, and her priorities pulling her in many directions: Tom's needs, Roger's wants, Jeff's desires, her career, the ordinary little crises of life. She wanted to close the doors and put a moratorium on everything until she could get herself in one piece again.

---

1. Why did Frannie feel that all of the right and wrong she had been taught was up for question after her divorce?

2. What caused Frannie to feel fragmented when she was sleeping with more than one lover?

3. Frannie felt it necessary to hide parts of her life from everyone. What effect would this secretiveness have on her development and her relationships?

Explaining Fragmentation

Fragmentation is related to splitting, but different in that the lover keeps herself or himself intact by keeping love and body together. The fragmentation stems from splitting loyalties. By caring personally for each lover, Frannie and other caring persons like Frannie feel a loyalty to each that cannot be fulfilled because the loyalties intrude upon each other. This results in distractedness and nervousness, which increase as the lovers overlap more closely in space or time. This is why Frannie became more upset when they all arrived in San Francisco. When they had been separated in both time and distance she had been far less aware of the inner conflict.

Effects of Sex Outside of Marriage

Bonding, Splitting, and Fragmentation: A Review

Although bonding is the natural result of sexual inter- course, this sometimes surprises the novice. And if there is no response to the bond, integrity is automatically lost because the body is in its most intimate experience while the mind and soul are aloof—not integrated into the intimacy. Thus, there is either an emotional bonding between two persons or an internal split between the body and emotions. A person may be unaware of the split at first because it happens slowly and does not initially create internal tension. On the other hand, the person who suffers fragmentation grows cognizant of it quickly, and so do friends, because the nervousness arising from inner tension becomes obvious. Since a person with overlapping lovers cares about each person and wants to keep herself or himself integrated, fragmentation is unavoidable and something one generally wants to escape. Like Harry with his long-term girlfriend and his new excitement, and Frannie with her various lovers converging in one place, persons in similar situations suffer fragmentation until a choice between lovers is made.

Sex before marriage means sex without total commitment. If this relationship does not involve deception, does not

73

result in disease or pregnancy, and does continue into marriage, the negative effects may be minimal. However, since engagement is a stressful time, when couples are adjusting to the idea of commitment, the added complication of sex can cause a split instead of a bond.

Decreased Potential for Intimacy

Once a person is past the first lover, several effects may be felt. First, each new lover decreases the potential for intimacy since personal intimacy is based on complete trust, openness, and the willingness to share one's feelings totally. Serial exclusiveness does not create the total split between body and emotion that nonrelational sex does, but it develops a pattern of restraint, a protective covering, which inhibits trust and openness. Each past lover diminishes one's freedom for sharing oneself with a new lover, so the difference between having had three lovers and thirteen is vast, but the greatest is between one and more than one.

The correlation between many lovers and a decreased potential for personal sharing is illustrated in Tom's story. Tom began quite early to realize he avoided personal intimacy. At sixteen, when Tom fell in love with Ellie, the loveliest girl in the church group, he tried to stop his unacceptable sex activities. He wanted to be faithful to Ellie, but when matters went wrong, the habit of escape was stronger than his desire to resist. Although Ellie never found out about the other girls, she sensed that he was holding back, not relaxed if the conversation became personal. His lack of willingness to be honest cost him the relationship, because Ellie had experienced true openness with other friends in the church group and knew something was missing in her relationship with Tom. She had tried to talk to Tom about openness, sharing her feelings and struggles with him, but Tom was certain that she would not understand if he shared his real self. He would turn the conversation to impersonal topics, plan an exciting date, make her laugh. Ellie loved being with Tom, but she wanted an openness that Tom would not give.

The hurt of ending the relationship with Ellie plunged Tom into an even greater need for the bolstering of his ego through sex.

Inhibition of Personal Development

Leaping from lover to lover without time for healing, time to become one's own self between lovers, also limits one's personal development. People remain in an adolescent state as long as they are actively engaged in the search, the courtship, and the honeymoon stages of a relationship. The energy and time needed year after year by those continually in new or unsettled relationships becomes a focus of life that deprives singles of the freedom to focus on the development of their gifts, ministries, careers, families, or whatever unique purposes for which each was created.

After a number of years, the constant focus on getting or keeping a lover becomes a life-style. Since emotions at the beginning of a love affair are much more intense than the companionship of committed relationships, the taste for something lasting fades. Falling in love and developing the initial stages of a relationship are self-centered times—necessary to establish an enduring relationship, but demanding. To go through a number of these in a row is debilitating. There is a time to take a hiatus from searching for a mate and get on with the life of giving, growing, and being.

All who use sex as a fix are avoiding growth in some area. Three of the disciplines essential to handling life's problems, according to M. Scott Peck in *The Road Less Traveled*, are: ability to delay gratification, dedication to the truth (including both honesty and knowledge of reality), and accepting responsibility for our own lives and actions. Nonrelational sex can inhibit growth in each of these areas.

Compromising Integrity

Last, many Christians involved in premarital or postmarital affairs are compromising their integrity. The need to deceive, lie, or be secretive about part of their lives results in a guardedness that clouds integrity. A low profile may be desirable, keeping people from being able to accept leadership in the church or to give themselves completely to God's call. Sometimes it seems necessary to compromise the truth when talking to family, children, or friends, because their expectations are different from the way the sexually active singles are living, and it seems easier to pretend than to openly examine the questionable life-style. This discrepancy between the pretended role and reality keeps the person from being integrated—and produces a sense of lost integrity.

---

1. What might have happened if Tom had told Ellie about his sex habits?
2. How does deception about sexual relationships— hiding situations from parents, friends, or church, or lying to them—affect a person's integrity? What might happen if singles who are sexually active were completely open?
3. Why do people need healing time between lovers?
4. How do the adaptations people make in sex relationships inhibit personal growth?

WHY SINGLES PURSUE SEX

*I*f singles are asked why they pursue sex apart from marriage, the answers will vary. It's fun, natural, a need; it keeps a relationship going; it's the only way to get a date; it's expected; it's a way to say "thank you"; it shows caring; or, it says that I love him or her. The sexually active who realize that they have an underlying need to prove something are freer to move into celibacy because they can evaluate the effect of their experiences and realize that better ways to meet those needs may exist. Those whose motives are hidden from themselves are more likely to continue the same patterns. Almost all of the sexually active are ignorant of the emotional effects of sexual intercourse.

Sex for Fun

The myth that sex can be indulged in for fun alone with no serious consequences is amazingly strong—among singles and those married, among religious people as well as secular. In spite of the pain, confusion, and dissatisfaction that we hear from the sexually active, the belief persists. Perhaps it is the intensity of the memory of the moment that blanks out the afterthoughts; or perhaps it is the strength of the media, which perpetuates the image; or perhaps it is simply a childlike hope that pleasure is obtainable without responsibility. Whatever the reason, sex for fun seems to have become part of the American dream. Jill believed in the myth that sex for fun poses no harmful consequences.

Jill and the Myth

Twenty-year-old Jill had just arrived at the training center for a two-month job orientation, away from her hometown in Kansas for the first time. She was attractive, confident, and eagerly looking forward to a great time in this new setting. When she entered the lounge on the first evening, she stood out as a fun person to get to know. As a group gathered to go out for dinner, Jill assessed the men. Pointing to a handsome blonde from Wyoming she announced, "You're tonight." Turning to each of the other three men under thirty, she stated, "You're tomorrow night. You're next, and you're next." Taking Number One's arm she led the way to dinner. The group looked at each other in amazement and amusement. "Does she mean what I think she means?" they asked each other.

Number One, David, happened to be a faithful husband and a father of two small girls; his faithfulness, however, did not withstand Jill's assault. Jill never moved on to Number Two.

Although Jill was simply out to have a good time, her emotions were not as sophisticated as her boldness implied, and the wild demands of eros hooked her with David. The intensity of the merger persisted through the training time until David had to decide whether to take a job back home or choose one in Oklahoma with Jill. The tension and anxiety exhausted Jill during those last two weeks while David was teetering. Her relief was immense when David opted for her and Oklahoma, but she soon found that the stress wasn't over. David continued vacillating throughout the next year as the pulls alternated in strength between his family and Jill. Both grief and release flooded Jill the day she came home from work to find all of David's belongings gone and a note saying that he had gone back to his wife and children.

Jill's Beliefs and Their Results

Jill thought of sex as fun, believing that she could go from man to man without any harm to anyone, experiencing momentary pleasure without any lasting feeling. Because people were away from home in a temporary setting, she thought what people did would have no effect on the rest of their lives.

But a marriage was permanently damaged; two children lost their father for a year, and David was tormented by tension, guilt, and indecision. David and Jill were trapped by an eros relationship that caused them to choose life-styles they did not want, to upset their families, and to be separated from their churches. Jill's emotional involvement detained her from happier relationships. Although Jill didn't mean for her actions to be harmful to anyone else, she rationalized and hid from the harm she was doing to David's wife and children. David knew the damage he was doing and was torn by it. Jill experienced hurt, loneliness, and a different path in life than she might otherwise have taken.

---

1. Why did Jill and David become emotionally bonded by one sexual incident, while many people have no sense of emotional tie in their experiences of casual sex?

2. Can a person be certain that he or she won't become bonded by the sex act?

3. How does Jill's experience demonstrate the difference between eros and agape?

Sex As a Symbol

Most people who have sex casually are using it as a substitute for something else. For many, sex symbolizes masculinity or femininity. For others, it can be interpreted to mean acceptance, desirability, self-worth, independence, freedom from some authority, or proof of almost anything. Most people do not examine their reasons, they simply accept the act as fun or natural—the accepted thing to do or way to relate. But looking at other people's reasons for being sexually active may give people more discernment in making appropriate choices for themselves.

Michael in Need

Michael was twenty-two years old, sexually untested, and in psychotherapy because his many fears kept him from dating. He seemed to be making no headway in therapy until a friend introduced him to an older woman of thirty who was willing to take him to bed in spite of his offensive manners. The transformation in Michael that resulted from one experience with sex was a release that therapy had not been able to achieve in months. The rigidity that had intruded into every attempt to date or relate to women had melted.

Michael's Beliefs and Their Results

Out of the many erroneous beliefs Michael held, two were germane to his problem. One, he believed that he would be impotent with a woman, and two, he believed that all women would reject him. The immediate effect of having these two incorrect and binding beliefs shattered was fantastic release because two paralyzing convictions had been proven false. This was a case where the truth set Michael free—the very limited truth that two fears were false, and so a very limited freedom. It would seem as though sex without love or commitment had been good for Michael in achieving his immediate goal; freedom from his inhibitions in relating initially to women.

The longer effects are uncertain, depending on which future actions and beliefs Michael chooses. Michael has begun the separation of sex and love, using a woman to meet his needs rather than loving her. Since he has successfully used sex to relieve some hurts, his temptation will be to continue to use sex as a fix, but he does not have to choose that way. If he continues in therapy and in association with loving people, he may learn to love. His release from his binding fears did not teach him anything about love or cure his objectionable manner of relating.

1. Was having sexual intercourse with Michael a loving act for that older woman to perform? Is the attempt to help someone through sex ever justifiable?

2. Could Michael have found release from his fears in another way?

3. How else might Michael's experience with this woman have turned out?

4. Michael's therapist had considered recommending a sexual experience, but refrained. How did this refrainment show wisdom?

Another reason that singles pursue sex is to find acceptance or at least to prove that they are acceptable. Sara's story exemplifies this need.

Sara the Virgin

Sara was in her third year of work in an office filled with women and had no social group that included eligible men. Even in the small high school she had attended there had been more girls than boys. At almost twenty-three she felt destined to be an old maid. Because Sara's contact with males had been extremely limited—only three dates in her whole life, no male friends, no brothers, and a father who had left the family before she was old enough to remember him—Sara was unaware of her attractiveness.

When Terry began flirting with Sara as he made deliveries to the office, she was at first surprised, next pleased, and then thrilled when he asked her to lunch. After the lunch date, Sara announced triumphantly to her best friend that Terry was taking her to the drive-in movies on Friday night.

Sara was concerned that Terry did not go to church, knowing that his values might be quite different from hers, but where else was she to meet a man? Because she wanted a date, longed for a boyfriend, and needed to know that she was attractive, Sara was vulnerable to the attention of any man.

81

Since Terry had a van, they didn't see much of the movie, and Sara's Christian values barely held against her warm, responsive nature. On the second date in the van, nature won, leaving Sara feeling very mixed: wiser and somehow vindicated, yet guilty and empty.

Knowing that she was not in love with Terry, and recognizing that this was not the kind of relationship she longed for, she refused to see him again.

Sara's Beliefs and Their Results

Sara believed that dating was necessary to prove her attractiveness as a woman. Thinking that all she had that could please a man was her body, Sara was afraid that Terry would reject her if she did not give him what he wanted, and his rejection would prove that she was not attractive to men.

She expected her job to be temporary, assuming that marriage and motherhood would be her career. It was God's job to provide her with the husband that would make this possible. Since she had been faithful to God, now God would be faithful to her in this one area where she needed help—a husband. But lately a tiny voice in Sara had begun to say, You're almost twenty-three in a dead-end job, with no men in your life. God has forgotten you.

Although Sara did not intend to lose her virginity, she didn't know her body, didn't know that there was a point of petting at which she would no longer be willing to say no.

Sara had quickly recognized the split between sex and love and realized that physical intimacy was not enough for her. She did not want her body involved again in a nonloving intimacy. She also realized that a blind hope for a husband was not going to fulfill her life; rather, she needed to scrutinize her career, her friendships, and her passive attitude toward life.

---

1. What items in Sara's belief system did you feel were incorrect? How?

2. How did Sara's beliefs about God affect her sexual behavior?

3. How can a passive attitude toward life be a detriment to a person's spiritual and personal development?

4. How did Sara turn this incident into a growth experience?

5. How could this experience have damaged Sara?

Some singles are afraid to know or develop themselves, as Cindy's story shows us.

Cindy the Divorcée

Cindy could not believe that she was divorced, that Andrew had left her for another woman. They both had been active in the church throughout their married lives, but after their two daughters married, Cindy had become even more active in the women's group, serving as coordinator for her circle. Now she highly resented the fact that she was going to have to get a job.

The memory that rankled most was Andrew's statement about the other woman: "She turns me on." Cindy had always thought herself to be quite capable in bed. Their sex life had pleased her until the last few months, when Andrew had become impotent occasionally, which she had just attributed to age. Now Andrew had implied that she was inadequate sexually. That stung. Proving herself sexually adequate seemed more important to Cindy than finding an appropriate career—more important, even, than following the rules of the church.

She had not dated during the separation, making sure that she was the wronged party. But after the divorce was final and his wedding date set, she needed somebody to ease her hurt and make her feel adequate again.

Frank, recently separated from his wife, came to Cindy's mind as she remembered how good his flattering compliments had always made her feel at the monthly church socials. Frank was pleased with the attention Cindy subsequently paid him and fell happily into a dating relationship with her. They both were experiencing the freshness of a new, uncluttered relationship—canoeing on the lake, throwing fish to the seals in the aquarium, listening to a symphony on the sofa, and picnicking on the beach with ample hugs and cuddling.

When Frank's business sent him to Dallas for two weeks, Cindy decided it was time for her to take a vacation. They agreed on separate rooms at the same hotel. During the first week Cindy felt vindicated when Frank assured her that she was very good in bed. Now she could convince herself that it wasn't really her fault that Andrew thought he needed another woman.

The friendship now bonded with sex, Cindy was transported into a comfortable euphoria, sure that her problems would be taken care of because she had a man. Eagerly she began planning for their future weeks and months together. Frank, however, still hoping for a reconciliation with his wife, was feeling stifled, and certainly wasn't ready to be tied so quickly.

Frank tried to let her down gently, encouraging her to date others and to pursue her interest in her career. Since they saw each other regularly in church, he didn't want a scene, but he told her that sex was out at home because it would be too complicated by their church friends and activities.

Cindy experienced a second rejection shortly after her divorce. Cindy was now tempted to plunge into a third relationship in order to ease the pain of the last rejection.

Cindy's Beliefs and Their Results

Cindy was using sex as a way to achieve what she thought she needed, assurance of her sexual attractiveness, and emotional and financial security. What she really wanted was a husband to fix her hurts and take care of her needs; it did not occur to her that she could take care of herself. Her whole orientation had always been that a man was necessary to take care of her emotionally, financially, and socially. In other words, a man was a sex object, not a person to relate to as a friend or as another equal human being. Cindy was also operating out of the conviction that sex is binding; therefore, getting a man in bed would give her a better chance of keeping him to take care of her.

Her church did not help to dispel these falsehoods. Even before her divorce was final, friends were trying to set her up with an attractive widower in the church. None of the couples invited her to social events with the couples she used to party with. No one talked about how to establish structure in her life—only, Who will the next man be?

The initial effect of the affair was stabilizing for Cindy. Some of the feelings of failure and unattractiveness caused by the divorce were dissolved when another man accepted her. However, at this stage of her development, because she expected a man to take care of her needs, Cindy did not try to deal with her pain or her fears of inadequacy. Nor did she feel the necessity to plan for herself her future in career, friendship, or finances since she was focused on finding a man who would take care of these matters for her.

If Cindy continues to abscond instead of dealing realistically with her problems, she will not develop those relational skills that would allow her freedom to have her needs met by people other than a husband or lover. By not examining those areas in which she is at fault for the marriage failure, she will not develop into a whole person. Again, the church tends to assign blame to one partner, causing the other to feel blameless. The necessity to maintain a blameless position can blind people to possibilities for growth. If she plunges into a second affair, she will again be trying to prove her adequacy by sex rather than by holding herself responsible for self-approval.

A hiatus from sex at this point could give her a new beginning on the journey toward wholeness.

---

1. What could motivate Cindy to want to develop herself and her abilities rather than spend her energy looking for men to take care of her?

2. What does the church do to contribute to beliefs that make women feel inadequate without husbands?

3. How does or could the church help to develop women and men who take their own responsibility for their emotional, social, and financial needs rather than expect another person to meet them all?

4. How do women view men as sex objects?

Tom the Helper

The reason Tom would probably give for his sex adventures outside of marriage is that he wants to help women. An examination of his life-style reveals other motives.

Tom found a spot in the lobby where he could watch people while he waited for Frannie. Six days ago he had seen Frannie, the daughter of his old college buddy, for the first time since her divorce. Frannie's father had thought that a night on the town with an older, sophisticated bachelor might cheer her up. Now, six days later, Tom knew that Frannie had fallen for him and would be pushing for marriage. He pondered how to handle this carefully without hurting Frannie, but keeping himself clear. Tom's Christian friends did not understand his rather casual attitude toward sex, and Frannie's father would certainly be shocked to discover that Tom's comfort had included bed.

It was typical of his friends, Tom mused, to expect him to have a healing effect on women. People had always been his primary interest, even though he had majored first in engineering, then had finished in business. His job as company representative for a machinery firm suited him perfectly. He understood machinery well, but he understood people even better.

He knew that he made a good impression in his business suit, his five-foot-ten frame still trim for his forty-five years. He rather liked the silver streaks that were appearing in his brown hair. Tom was an expert at gaining and keeping people's confidence. He had become the top representative in his company during his third year and had maintained that position for twenty years.

It had always been easy for Tom to gain the confidence of women too, so being a bachelor suited him. Tom did not consider himself promiscuous since he never thought of his affairs as using women. He truly liked each woman when he was with her; he just didn't want the responsibility or the limitation imposed by having only one. His college room-mate, who had become a pastor, periodically brought up the subject of "Tom's loose living," as he labeled Tom's life-style, but Tom could not see any damage done when his caring for a woman included sex.

He reflected on his many years of experience with women. Seldom did he pick women up at a singles' group or a bar—they were too easy. It was usually someone who needed help, like the red-eyed office girl he had chatted with while waiting to see that manager in Seattle, or the lonely career woman climbing the corporate ladder in Denver. His caring nature sought out these needy ones who weren't out looking. He was sincerely interested in their problems, truly desiring to make them feel alive and feminine. Didn't sex always make people feel better, ease tension, engender self-worth? he asked himself. It was his way of helping.

Tom considered the possibility of marrying Frannie and preserving the image of the great hero that he was to her at this moment. Several times lately young women had lapped up his careful listening, but had seemed shocked at his sexual advances. The young and beautiful Frannie's wholehearted response had been gratifying; he was afraid, however, that he couldn't maintain that facade of constant thoughtfulness indefinitely. It was fun for a few days, but wearing, even for the week he had been here. Since Tom prided himself on being the great helper of many, tying himself to one even as charming as Frannie would inhibit his joy of helping other needy women. Besides, he rather enjoyed his bachelor life-style with many women feeding his need for adoration. At forty-five, he would have to be pressured to change his patterns.

Tom's Beliefs and Their Results

Tom assumed that sex was restorative—relieving body tension, making people feel better about themselves, and giving hope. God must approve of his giving so much love and help to women. As long as he made each woman feel good, Tom believed that his behavior couldn't be wrong.

His own self-worth was heavily tied to being the great lover-helper. When his listening skills were accepted but his body was not, Tom felt rejected. On the other hand, Tom believed that a woman would not accept his body unless he were constantly attentive. Knowing he had women in his territory who would at any time welcome him into their beds was a big part of Tom's security.

Tom thought that he could not be faithful to one woman, that he needed freedom to be his whole self and to use all of his gifts.

Tom had developed his relating skills of friendliness, listening, and light conversation highly, so he was in great demand for dinner parties and socials. His skills as a short-term lover, also highly developed, gave him entrance to many bedrooms where he provided momentary pleasure to lives.

Although Tom thought he was loving in his sexual encounters with women, he had actually split sex from love. He would not take responsibility for a relationship with any woman, wanting only the brief touch, not the sharing of life. Since Tom's listening and lover skills were perfected so well and his time with any one woman was short enough that his attentiveness did not wane, he left a woman with a model no man—not even Tom himself—could match in a continuing relationship. Many women hoped for a future with him, rejected men with less polish, or lived in frustration with husbands who appeared in their minds to have lesser skills of caring.

Tom had become addicted to adoration from many women. He had perfected the initial relating skills, but had no knowledge of deeper sharing or responsible love. Personal intimacy was impossible for Tom because his life-style required hiding from everyone. Evading truth became so much a part of his life that he lied even to his friends who knew better. The intense pleasure of quick gratification for his body and adoration for his soul had denied him intimate love and growth into a genuinely loving person.

---

1. What is the most serious misconception of Tom's beliefs?
2. What aspects of sharing deeply did Tom not experience because of his constant short-term affairs?
3. In what ways would Tom's life be different if he used his listening-caring skills but remained celibate?
4. What will happen to Tom ten years from now?

Gina: Trapped with Children

Gina's experience is extremely common in this day of easy divorce. Gina met Joe, a car salesman, at a Parents Without Partners meeting. She was delighted to discover that he didn't mind having kids around. With a seven-year-old, a five-year-old, and a limited income from her job as a clerk, Gina had found meeting men difficult. Baby-sitting was expensive, and finding a man who liked to be around kids was beginning to seem impossible.

She really wanted to find someone who was willing to spend time around the house so she could share some of the burden and have some time with her kids. Marriage is what she needed, but next best was a live-in who would share some of the expenses and responsibility.

Joe played with the kids and seemed to enjoy dates that included them. He didn't mind eating at the house and watching TV after the kids were in bed; he would even occasionally pay for a baby-sitter when Gina wanted to go out with him. Gina was happy to compensate him with her charms in bed, hoping to hold him and perhaps, eventually, marry him.

At first Gina did not object to the weekends Joe took off on "business trips." She was so delighted to have someone around, even part of the time, and so fearful of losing him, that she made no demands. Eventually she acknowledged to herself that there were other women in Joe's life, but she just hoped that she would win out.

It was almost a year before she realized that she had not met anyone in Joe's life, no one from work, none of his family, none of his friends. By accident she found out that he had taken another woman to the banquet where he had received the top salesman award. When she faced him with his duplicity, he stated that he had never promised her fidelity and that he had a perfect right to date whomever he pleased. Indignantly she told him to take everything and leave.

However, the bonding was too strong and the good times too pleasurable to end so easily. Joe called to ask about the kids and they cautiously moved into the comfortable pattern again. Gina hoped that his coming back meant fidelity, but she didn't ask until she found out about a family wedding she had not been invited to.

The relationship became more and more frustrating until Joe left and refused to come back, but even then Gina kept on hoping.

Gina's Beliefs and Their Results

Gina felt the need of a man for companionship and security. Giving herself sexually was compensation for his attention and a way to keep him. She believed that her need for companionship was greater than her own or her children's needs for a life-style in harmony with her old values.

Gina's children had become very attached to Joe, so when he left she not only risked her own feelings of rejection but also her children's. By relying on Joe, she was not building alternative ways to meet her companionship and security needs. This influenced her to seek another live-in when Joe left. She was modeling for her children a life-style of dependency on men, of mutual using, of nonmarriage, and of uncertainty. She was putting her children in the social position of having to acknowledge their mother's life-style by all the references they made to Joe.

Gina's sexual involvement prolonged the affair, consuming time that she could have been using to build her own resources and healthier relationships.

---

1. What does it do to young children for a divorced parent to have a live-in lover?
2. What might a celibate single woman with young children and a limited income do for a social life?
3. Would Gina have been wiser to ignore the other women in Joe's life?

The bonding effect of sex provides the basis for the majority of singles' reasons for pursuing sex: acceptance, belonging, keeping a lover, feeling adequate, and other acceptance-belonging types of needs. The intense momentary pleasure serves as the motivator for the experience-seeking people. Most singles simply accept sex as a part of their lives without examining their motives too closely or considering the consequences for the future.

5

WHY SINGLES REMAIN CELIBATE

*R*easons for celibacy among singles lie on a continuum. On one end is fear, then lack of opportunity, then discipline because it is right, and finally, at the opposite end, a true understanding of love of God, others, and self. Like motives for many behaviors, reasons for celibacy within most individuals are mixed, and vacillating along the continuum occurs. Since celibates come in a variety of styles, illustrated below are a variety of motives and their effects.

Celibacy from Fear

Fear has always been a strong motivator for keeping women celibate. Almost the only reasons most parents can give children for maintaining virginity stem from fear. Fear of the physical consequences and fear of what people would say have been strong, but the strongest have been the generalized, unnamed fears instilled in early childhood, and the threat of withdrawal of love. Frannie and Lori experienced these fears.

Frannie and Lori: The Fearful

As far back as Frannie could remember, her Christian mother had sniffed at "immoral girls" who had become pregnant. Her first sexual information had been associated with what those bad girls do. In high school she had been called a prude because of her shock when she discovered that any of her friends were "playing with fire." Being a pleaser at heart, Frannie was torn between wanting to please a boyfriend and the terror of her father's cold judgment if she ever became pregnant.

In college, when her fiancé's demands became overwhelming, Frannie discovered that she could keep him satisfied by using her mouth and hands, while maintaining her own technical virginity. Anxiety kept her from even desiring an orgasm; all she wanted was to feel loved, please Clay, and keep from becoming an "immoral girl." As we noted in chapter 3 Frannie didn't experience orgasm in her marriage either.

Lori's mother, like Frannie's, had begun warning Lori about "those things boys want to do to you" when Lori entered junior high. Lori eyed boys from a safe distance in the corridors and around the lockers, fearing for the safety of the girls who teased, chased, and were pursued by boys, yet longing to be part of the fun. Finding two other shy girls, she formed a tight clique, never nearing the boys.

Secretly, Lori longed for a boyfriend, but she blushed scarlet and stammered if a boy she liked looked her way, dashing off to the safety of her girlfriends. When a boy in her world history class at high school asked her to go to a movie, she stared in dumb shock, remembering "what boys' hands do at movies." Before she could think what to say, the boy muttered, "Well, I'm not trying to rape you!" turned in disgust, and walked away. Relieved, Lori dashed to her girlfriends to relay the news.

After high school, Lori's nursing career made it easy to stay quietly in a feminine world. At twenty-five she had never had a date, never known a boy or man as a friend, and was sadly adjusting her life to a totally female-oriented existence.

---

1. How can parents encourage abstinence without making sex seem dirty?
2. How could Lori begin seeing men as persons rather than as sex objects?

3. How do oral sex and mutual masturbation affect a courtship?

4. What relationship was there between Frannie's satisfying her fiancé before marriage and her lack of orgasm during sexual intercourse after marriage?

Celibacy from Idealism

The emphasis in churches on God's "perfect will" can give fuel to already idealistic young people, creating either a superior attitude or anxiety.

Ed the Idealist

Some singles seem to feel smug in their celibacy, giving an impression that everything in their lives—especially romance—will be done perfectly, without deviation from a storybook ideal. Their interpretation of the loving Father who directs our paths seems to imply that no suffering, no mistake, no risk can befall them. Ed gave this impression.

Ed sat in the back row of the singles' class, arms folded, surveying the crowd. His eyes narrowed thoughtfully as a vivacious girl with blond hair took the mike on the platform. He nodded as she announced a hike planned for the following Friday evening—his kind of woman. At thirty-three and never married, he had reviewed the assets of many women, dated some until they failed to live up to some point on his checklist, and had mildly lost his heart to two—both now married to other men.

As the meeting closed, a smiling woman approached Ed. He looked down, pretending to be absorbed in finding something in his wallet, turned the other direction, and walked toward the blonde. The no-longer-smiling woman shrugged as she scanned the room for more promising contacts. Ed had already checked her off: too old, she must be thirty-five at least. Ed edged through the crowd surrounding the blonde, whose attention appeared to be focused on a young "hot shot"—who couldn't be over twenty-five. A slightly overweight brunette called for Ed's help in collecting books. Reluctantly he grabbed a few books, impatient to get back to his pursuit of the blonde.

Ruby, the brunette, cheerfully kidded him about his reluctance to help. Ed glanced her way but did not bother to answer. She, too, had been crossed off the list: not classy enough. She was a good worker, okay for a few laughs, but not his type, not worth spending time on.

Ed prided himself on his virtue, keeping aloof from women. He would wait for the perfect one for him, then give all of his love and virility. Living alone, absorbed in his work, playing his weekly game of golf, and attending church and the singles' group on Sunday satisfied his life with order as he waited to discover the perfect woman. Finishing with the book pickup, he again aimed toward the blonde, and eventually succeeded in talking with her. So it went—and so went other encounters with other just-less-than-satisfactory women.

Ed was thirty-four when he fell in love. It had not been easy for him to remain celibate all of those years, but Ed was an idealist. Since he had chosen, wooed, and won his wife-to-be, and she was wearing his engagement ring, now sex was finally right. The weekend in Carmel was like a premature honeymoon—long hours on the beach, back to the motel; wandering through little shops, back to the motel. But a misunderstanding developed, growing beyond their ability to communicate, climaxing in a breakup, and Ed stormed away.

Quickly Ed turned to another lover since his celibacy had been broken, his idealism—that perfect, storybook relationship he had imagined—had been smashed, and he was very hurt. By the time his ex-fiancée called to try to repair the damage, the new lover was pregnant.

Ed's Beliefs and Their Results

Sex belonged with one woman only and when the commitment was made he believed sex was right. When Ed was hurt, he believed all was lost. His pride blinded him from seeing how to work out what seemed to him an unforgivable situation.

Since emotions run high during engagement, and couples test each other at this time, adding sex made Ed much more vulnerable to hurt. His disillusionment made him feel like a fool—and act like one.

---

1. What is wrong with having a checklist?
2. How do fear and pride relate to Ed's idealism?
3. Why is idealism so dangerous?
4. What are the risks of sex during engagement?

Celibacy Through Busy-ness

Some singles remain chaste because they have worked out techniques that keep them out of temptation. Barbara's methods worked, although she stumbled onto them accidentally.

Barbara the Busy

Barbara had used sex for a brief time after her divorce to make her feel adequate while she was adjusting to a sense of failure and rejection, but she found nonrelational sex unfulfilling. Not wanting to become emotionally involved again for awhile, she focused on her career. However, since her married boss attracted her immensely, she wondered how she could keep from succumbing to his overtures. Pretending appointments when he invited her for a quick drink after work established a work-oriented relationship with him. Actually making appointments with friends kept her mind occupied and did not allow her time to wonder what she was missing by not accepting his suggestions. As Barbara became familiar with the work setting and her mind was increasingly occupied with advancement in her job, she found herself thinking less and less about her boss's attractiveness. Outside of work, she had activities for each evening of the week, so no time was available for thinking about him.

Late one afternoon, while she and her boss were involved in a work project, he suggested that they continue brainstorming over a cup of coffee at the lunch counter next door. She accepted without thinking about their relationship because she was so absorbed in the project. She found herself able to concentrate on work, thoroughly enjoy him in this setting, and not feel vulnerable to falling into bed. How encouraging to discover, she thought, that the intense feeling of attraction can diminish when it is ignored for awhile.

The strategies that Barbara used to avoid a sexual relationship with her boss included (1) avoiding tempting situations while she knew she was vulnerable—especially anything involving alcohol, which would lower her resistance; (2) focusing on her career; and (3) keeping busy in activities that she enjoyed.

---

1. What other methods can alleviate one's unwanted attraction to another without avoiding the person?
2. Is there any value in friendship between a man and a woman if marriage is not a goal?
3. Was Barbara flirting with danger to see her boss, a married man, away from the office?
4. Could Barbara continue to work with him outside the office without being tempted to have an affair?

Celibacy by Accident

Jeri had always been the "nice girl" in the church group, but there comes a time. . . .

Jeri the Frustrated

As the door closed on the last couple leaving the party, Jeri burst out to her friend, "Roxanne, how could you?"

Astonished, Roxanne retorted, "How could I what?"

"Make such a big deal out of my thirtieth birthday—black crepe paper, announcing my age to the world, all those jokes about being an old maid. Roxanne, how could you?" The tears oozed out as Jeri slumped down at the kitchen table.

Roxanne's eyes met those of Alan, her husband, and then sought affirmation from Linda, the other single who had stayed. Alan shrugged while Linda rolled her eyes in resignation.

Alan began, "After all, Jeri, Roxanne and Linda put in a lot of work . . . "

"I know, I know, I'm sorry. I don't want to seem unappreciative. It's just that you all knew how upset I've been about turning thirty," Jeri apologized.

"But we're all over thirty," Roxanne stated. "What we wanted was to make a joke so you would get over this ridiculous idea of being so old!"

"But you're married. You have a year-old child. If I don't find someone soon, it'll be too late. Life will have passed me by." Suddenly she looked at Linda, remembering that Linda was thirty-eight, unmarried, with no children. "Oh, Linda, I'm sorry. Everything I say is wrong tonight. I'm just not thinking. You do just fine being single. You love your career, you're active in all kinds of stuff. I really admire you. It's okay for you not to have a husband or children because you're stronger than most women. I'm different; I need someone to build my life with, a family, the traditional things. I can't imagine me being thirty-eight without a child. It's okay for you, but not me."

"It was on my thirty-second birthday that I went through what you're going through," Linda replied. "I thought that I couldn't be a whole woman without a child. The pain would hit me periodically—when I was discouraged, feeling low about my job, a friend had disappointed me, or on milestone occasions like New Years or birthdays. But overall, the amount of time that I actually spent being immobilized or deeply saddened about not having a child was minimal—maybe a few hours a year. Now I have no desire to have a baby. I love spending a few hours playing auntie to Roxanne's and Alan's sweetie-pie, but I'm equally thankful to let them take over the twenty-four-hour haul. I don't miss having a ten- or fifteen-year-old around the house either. Oh, if it had happened, I would have loved it because I would have adjusted. But, Jeri, God has made us adaptable creatures."

"I don't want to hear that. It's like giving up—accepting second best. I don't want to adapt. I want a baby. Maybe I'll meet somebody on my Caribbean trip."

It was a month later when a much calmer Jeri shared her vacation experience with Roxanne. She had met Jim on the third day of the two weeks in the Bahamas. The attraction had been mutual and they had spent many hours openly sharing their lives and feelings. Although Jim had a girlfriend back home, Jeri thought that the intensity of their relationship would obliterate Jim's ties. She was determined to make this man be the one. Moving to New York and leaving her career, friends, and family were no problem for Jeri. Her objective was marriage, now, before it was too late to have a family.

The desire to cement their intense feelings with sexual intimacy was nearly overwhelming. However, the logistics of the Bahama situation—the family she was staying with, the friends he was with—allowed almost no privacy and would have made the sexual union awkward and hasty. So it was a regretful Jeri who reported to Roxanne that there had been no sexual fulfillment. The last night had been a dream with promises to write, visit, and maybe plan for a future.

As Jeri settled into her old life-style again, appreciating her apartment, busy in her round of activities, and enjoying her friends, she began to wonder if she would really love being in New York so much. When she called Jim one evening and found his girlfriend there, she was furious. It was not until later that Jeri became tremendously relieved that she had not left a piece of herself with Jim. Much later, when Jim called to let her know that he was marrying the girl back home, she was also glad that he didn't have a cloud on his relationship with his new wife.

Jeri's Beliefs and Their Results

Jeri was convinced that she could not be a whole person without being a mother. She was aware that sex with Jim would have put the relationship on a different footing; more would be at stake for her. She would have undergone more bonding and, as a result, would be more vulnerable to feelings of rejection. She also believed that five, ten, and twenty years from now her wants would be the same.

Contemplating major changes in her life (moving to New York and marriage) made Jeri more content with her present life. After she had been home awhile, she was relieved that she had not bonded herself sexually with Jim, even though she had initially been sad. She examined Linda's life a little more carefully and discovered that it was fully as satisfying as the lives of the thirty-eight-year-old married women whom she knew. Although this did not take away the desire to marry or have children, it eased the fear.

---

1. How might Jeri and Jim have each been different if they had slept together?

2. Can you think of examples of how desires change at different stages of life? What does this tell us about putting off certain experiences that we want now?

3. What was it in Jeri's belief system that made thirty such a traumatic birthday?

4. What made Jeri more content with her life after the Bahamas?

Celibacy for Ministry

Some singles are so absorbed in their careers, hobbies, or the work for God they are called to, that they spend little time thinking about sexual possibilities. If they do experience a longing for marriage or sex, they seldom want to spend the time it takes to develop relationships. This is a very useful kind of celibacy that frees them to pursue callings that they feel are important. (However, the freedom to pursue callings to ministry could also be freedom for selfish pursuits. This use of celibacy would not cultivate a socially healthy individual.)

Ken the Dedicated

Ken had been a visionary all of his life. Always he seemed to find new dreams to work on. After finishing his degree in dentistry, he decided that he could do more for people as a social worker. With a doctorate in social work, he could accomplish even more for people, he thought, but what about theology? Perhaps he could combine theology and social work and even more broaden his influence. And so he launched out into further postgraduate study.

In the midst of working toward these degrees, his heart was pulled by the plight of delinquent boys—another dream, a halfway house for homeless juveniles who had been in trouble with the police. As each dream grew, his load of responsibility became heavier, and the time that he might have spent seeking a wife was consumed in earning and raising money for the boys' home he had begun or commuting to his job as a college professor or speaking to promote one of his dreams.

By age forty-five, Ken had been talking about marriage for over ten years. Yet he continually made choices that eliminated the time needed for courting, and made his life more difficult to share. He could not imagine a woman with the education and cultural interests he would require in a wife, one content to live in a halfway house and counsel delinquent boys.

101

Ken seemed to gain energy from all of his contacts. The boys gave him family, the professorship gave him status, the theology gave him contacts to further his dreams, and his relationship to God gave him the satisfaction of knowing that his life counted for something. Keeping busy kept Ken from having much time to reflect on wanting a wife.

Ken is an exciting man, who gives off all the male vibes a woman could want, and longs for the intimacy of marriage, but he abstains from sexual involvement for moral reasons. To Ken, it would be irresponsible, debilitating, and entangling to involve himself with a woman unless she were the one he planned to marry. He hopes some day to marry some unique woman who will give him comfort and encouragement without withholding him too much from his dreams and projects. But sometimes the call to ministry simply doesn't leave room for a satisfactory marriage also.

Ken's Beliefs and Their Results

Ken believes that he has unique opportunities and abilities to perform service for the people God has called him to. He has an unusually high sense of responsibility, believing that purity in body and mind are necessary to please God and to accomplish his work. Discipline has a high priority for Ken.

Ken's ministry is too demanding for him to spend the time usually required for a successful courtship. Unless God intervenes unusually, it is unlikely that Ken will marry. However, he has friends everywhere, both men and women; he commands respect personally and professionally; and his social life is so active that he needs his home as a place to collapse. Perhaps he is truly called to singleness—at least for this period of his life.

---

1. Does Ken have more energy for ministry because he is celibate?
2. Is it true that it would take a woman of very unusual qualifications to be Ken's wife?

3. If Ken married, would his long celibate wait make it unlikely that he could have a good sexual relationship with his wife?

4. Would marriage make Ken's life more satisfying than it now is?

Possible Effects of Celibacy—Temporary and Long-Term

Since celibacy is refraining from and not carrying out a desirable action, the primary effect of celibacy is self-discipline. The celibate who has been tempted toward the sexually active camp but has refrained is developing the ability to delay gratification. M. Scott Peck in *The Road Less Traveled* emphasizes that delayed gratification is one of the basic tools required for dealing effectively with life's problems. Discipline is also essential to the Christian, and a fruit of the Holy Spirit (Gal. 5:23). Abstinence promotes this virtue.

Secondarily, some things do not happen to us that might if we did not refrain, and we may retain options or freedoms that the noncelibate gives up. For example, we may be

— free from fear of pregnancy and venereal disease
— free from social-family-church disapproval
— free to enter new romantic relationships without entanglements
— free from the split between body and emotions
— freer to experience a spiritual "one flesh" in marriage

Although we have the opportunity to keep our internal unity of body, mind, and emotion—that is, not split the body from emotions as the sex-for-fun people do—celibacy does not create integration. The split can occur in fantasy also. Physical celibacy without mental celibacy does not guarantee integration.

However, celibacy does make possible an unclouded

spiritual experience of the "one flesh" in marriage that Genesis 2:24 refers to. But, again, celibacy before marriage does not guarantee the feeling of unity, since it is the mind and will that must operate for that total union to be realized; but having no shadows of other bodies may help to cement love and sex, the bonding process. When both partners are virgins, they need not worry about not being as good as someone else in the past. No memories of better performances are stored to invade the mind or tempt one to infidelity.

Another, more subtle effect of celibacy is the freedom to develop intimacy with people and to experience the emotions of love, appreciation, and joy without the stimulus of sex. Pastors, priests, and psychologists often develop trusting relationships, which allow a deep intimacy of sharing because the roles are clearly established. Once celibacy is established between two persons, they are free to drop the posturing inherent in the sex roles accepted in our society. Then it becomes possible to explore other aspects of the personalities, and even necessary, if the relationship is to continue. Sexual excitement is such a strong emotion that it disguises the more subtle feelings, even as the bright colors of a coastal region blind one initially to the pastel hues of the desert. It takes time for the eye to discern the faint salmons, turquoises, mauves, and ochres in what at first seemed to be only beige and gray. So when one's focus in male-female relationships turns away from sex, a broader spectrum of the person can come into view.

Another often unnoticed effect of abstinence is a greater freedom from sexual desire than the sexual indulger experiences. Persons who have been sexually active find that their bodies initially make strong demands for orgasm, and that even after as much as six months or a year they are still very vulnerable to sexual advances. However, the body's desire gradually decreases, giving one much more freedom in relationships. Since the sex drive is so dominated by the habits of the mind, this decrease is only apparent if mental celibacy accompanies the physical abstinence.

Motives for Celibacy Determine the Effects

The Effect of Fear

Although fear is seldom given as a reason for abstinence, it is often an underlying motive. With realistic fears such as venereal disease and other genuine risks, one can weigh the pros and cons and make a valid choice. But with some of the hidden doubts—fear of inadequacy, fear of hurt, fear of responsibility, and more—one may use God as a cover and not deal with the fears. The effect we see in the person, then, comes from the fear rather than chastity. Fear's effects are limiting and binding: anger, withdrawal, paralysis, and jealousy, to name a few. Some people cannot bear to lose control, which makes a frightening prospect of that momentary vulnerability that occurs when giving oneself sexually. The characteristics often attributed to "old maids" are owing more to fear and bitterness than to celibacy.

The Effect of Legalism

Another cause for celibacy is the insurance some young men and women expect to receive by making deals with God. "If I stay pure," they bargain with God, "then I expect you to give me . . . " Usually the expectation is an ideal spouse. Sometimes these young (or not so young) persons do nothing to develop their abilities to exercise agape-love, never learn the skills of friendship, withdraw selfishly into their cubicles, and wait for God to ignore all of the principles of relationships that he has established and dump them into the "perfect" marriage because they were celibate. Celibacy is neutral, providing options and space for the development of good relationships, but not creating a relationship. Some abstainers keep the rules hoping to get a reward, but the usual reward is not to pay the penalty for breaking the rule. So they don't get herpes, but they don't form relationships either. Pride, idealism, and condemnation of others are often results of a legalistic attitude.

The Effect of Believing That It Is Healthy

The freedom that comes from abstinence combined with a willingness to develop loving relationships is the most desirable position. A commitment to abstinence deters us from using people, but agape-love takes risks, and people who take risks are exciting. If those celibates will learn to experience the persons in their lives with care and interest; if they will use the freedom of time, choice, and money to develop their interests, talents, and ministries; and if they will choose a healthy view of themselves, they have the option of living fulfilled lives.

---

1. What are the advantages and disadvantages of abstaining from sex outside of marriage?
2. What advantages does a permanent celibate such as a priest or nun have?
3. The sex drive diminishes as the habit of occupying the mind with other things grows. Why might this be frightening to some people?
4. Why do some celibates reap little reward for their abstinence?
5. What are the rewards for a loving celibate?

6

THE NEED FOR HEALING

*A*dult singles face questions and decisions that those following the expected path do not have to cope with. Because of the lack of societal structure for singles and an ignorance of what is helpful, we tend to act in ways that result in harm. We are also victims of the ignorance or attitudes of those around us. This can leave us with a need to be healed, or at least a need to interpret our lives in healthy ways.

Growing

We have followed Frannie's struggles through a healing process, and have seen that Tom's attitudes haven't changed much from early adolescence to middle age. Here is the last episode of Frannie and Tom.

Frannie the Experienced

Frannie had found it terribly hard to tell Tom that she was through sleeping with him. The timing couldn't have been worse. Frannie sensed that Tom was finally, at fifty-one, ready to settle down, and he had chosen her. He had obviously been puzzled by her reticence since she had been consistently accepting and eager to please before. But "before" had been one- or two-night stands when she could clear her calendar and be completely devoted to him; he had never been part of her regular life. Now, living in San Francisco where the other men in Frannie's life had converged, she was caught in trying to please too many.

When Frannie had finally realized she could not be loyal to more than one man, she had settled on Jeff as the one. She knew that Jeff had not slept with anyone else since their first time together, which had eventually made her uncomfortable in her infidelity. Jeff wasn't as experienced as Tom in lovemaking, and it was hard for Frannie to limit herself to Jeff alone and miss the sensual pleasures of Tom. She was also terribly frustrated by choosing not to comfort Tom with sex when she knew that sex boosted his ego and he so desperately needed encouragement at this trying time in his career.

Once, after Frannie had told him that it was over, she did end up in bed with Tom; habit was strong. But her feeling of disloyalty to Jeff and her fear of hurting him brought her back to her earlier resolve.

As she and Jeff became closer and Frannie wanted to share more of herself with Jeff, she wondered about introducing Jeff to Tom. She had casually mentioned an old family friend down on his luck that she had lunch with occasionally, but had feared for the two of them to meet.

When Tom had a heart attack, Jeff couldn't understand the depth of Frannie's concern or her feeling of responsibility. This was a part of her life that she only dared share superficially with Jeff, even though they were now talking of marriage. It was especially touchy since she had once called Jeff "Tom" during a moment of special intimacy. Her explanations had left Jeff unconvinced and hurt.

Sometimes Frannie found herself comparing Jeff to Roger, too. Roger's quick wit had made lovemaking particularly delightful to Frannie, while Jeff's ponderous ways could frustrate her to anger on occasion. Only once had she made a remark aloud in irritation, but that was enough to undermine Jeff's security once more. Yet Jeff made her feel more loved and cherished than she had ever felt before.

How Frannie longed to be able to be completely open with Jeff! But what she had revealed had created such insecurity that she dared not reveal more. She had nothing she could give Jeff that she hadn't already given to other men, except her fidelity. She could think of no way she could prove him most special except with time and continued loyalty. She hoped that the comparisons would eventually be wiped out of her mind so she could give herself more completely when she was with him.

Frannie's Beliefs

Frannie had in the past believed that giving sex was giving love. Now she believed that giving fidelity was giving love. She felt that the sex-love that she had given in the past obligated her to try to help Tom, even though she had no commitment to him. She also hoped that with time and fidelity, she could wipe out the intensity of the past memories that interfered with her total giving of herself to Jeff.

Evaluating Frannie's and Tom's Experiences

Giving sex to Tom resulted in two difficulties for Frannie; one, she had to withdraw love and support when he most needed it, and two, sex with an exceptionally accomplished lover diminished her ability to be satisfied in a love relationship with Jeff. Her sexual intimacies with other lovers made it seem necessary to withhold truth about herself from Jeff, at least temporarily, depriving both of them of the joy of total openness. Her experiences caused Jeff to feel insecure, which also created a little island of fear to walk around.

We have seen Frannie grow from a fearful teenager, survive a devastating divorce, grasp after a first lover, understand herself as not wanting casual sex, learn to give herself in love, become fragmented by overlapping lovers, and finally understand the necessity of fidelity and commitment to one lover. Although Frannie experienced much pain in her search, she continued to risk and allowed the pain to point her toward the truth of how God made humans to operate best.

Tom, on the other hand, made very little change in his value system from his early teens, when he discovered sex as a fix, to age fifty-one, when he had his heart attack. He did

109

not allow the pain he felt with Ellie to change his course, probably because he was too successful in obtaining other things he wanted. His continued success in supporting his ego, his ability to live without complete openness to anyone, and his lack of awareness of the pain he caused many of his lovers by presenting an impossible hope, kept him from needing to make any change. Now, if he recovers from his heart attack, he has the option to live the richest part of his life. Although he has lost Frannie, his awareness of the need to settle with one woman can lead him to responsible love, delayed gratifications, and the joy of knowing that he can be accepted by a woman when he is relaxed and not continually attending to her wants. The best may be ahead for both Tom and Frannie if they are willing to deny themselves easy gratification and set themselves on the course of responsible love.

---

1. Why might Frannie have chosen Jeff even though past lovers had better lovemaking techniques?

2. Would Frannie have been able to be more loving to Tom when he had his heart attack if she had never been his lover?

3. Was Frannie wise in not sharing all of her past with Jeff?

4. Which of Frannie's beliefs about love is more accurate, and why?

Getting Stuck

People choose behavior based on what they believe is best for them. By the same token, they are not likely to alter their behavior patterns unless the belief systems underlying these patterns change first—and some beliefs are so hard to dislodge that people who hold them find themselves stuck in a damaging life-style. Let's look at some of these beliefs.

110

Those hooked on the don't-use-it-lose-it theory can be sure that this is not true. Any large church can produce many cases of men and women who have been celibate into their thirties and older, as well as those previously married but celibate between marriages for many years, who have had perfectly normal and enjoyable sex relations when they married. We also know of married and sexually active men who become impotent and of married women who have no orgasms. Therefore, abstaining from sex for long periods of time is not a determining factor in sexual performance or enjoyment.

Young virgins can get stuck in the damaging belief that a girl cannot keep her boyfriend if she does not become involved in sexual arousal. Although men in the habit of sex may not continue dating without it, many men have their own values. Knowing men as friends can develop into good relationships, even while they are "dating" others. Many times a friendship can become a better marriage than those marriages based on the kind of dating that demands sexual using. Many young women accept sex as inevitable because they believe that having a series of "boyfriends" whom they have sex with gives them more worth, or increases their chances of happiness, than a series of "friends" whom they can enjoy and grow with. In the long run, friendships are more rewarding.

Another combination of beliefs that keep women in continuous sexual relationships was exemplified in chapter 4 by Gina, the divorcée with the young children. Women like Gina, who believe that marriage is the primary goal in life and must be accomplished before one can get on with the lesser objectives, continue in the one-at-a-time category until they find a husband. The belief in the primacy of marriage, combined with the conviction that sex is binding, motivates such a woman to get a man into bed so that he will feel obligated to marry her. For some men sex does increase obligation to the relationship, often depending on how responsible they feel for initiating the act. Especially inexperienced men may find her initiative an easier route to comfort than going out and searching the field. Since the narrower the goal the more likely one is to achieve it, these

111

women often succeed in marrying, even if it takes several tries to find a man who feels sufficiently obligated.

Although their goal of marriage is obtained, God's goals of discipline and trust may not have been attained, and marriage does not wipe out the results of manipulation, fear, and compromise that will affect their relationship, families, and ministry.

Another motivating belief is that all the glamour the media connect with sex might be real. If so, then one is missing out on the greatest pleasure of life if one abstains from sex; one cannot be whole if one is not participating in the great American pastime. Singles motivated by this belief move into sex out of fear of losing out or desire to satisfy themselves. The underlying American "me-ism" comes out strongly in the sexual realm. "I need to be fulfilled. I need to express myself. I am being thwarted, denied, unsatisfied." All of these attitudes lead to viewing sex as one's right, a means of experiencing oneself rather than a commitment to become one flesh with another person, willing to love that other as one's own flesh. These experiences often bring momentary pleasure, but the effect, as we have seen, is to weaken the habits of discipline and responsible love that can bring lasting character and richness to life.

 ## Getting Healed

The first step in getting healed is to wipe out these false beliefs and put truth in their place. The basic truth that those continuing in promiscuous sex need to internalize is that they are acceptable without this constant proving of themselves. What a relief it is to be freed from the immense amount of time and energy it takes to continually find new partners!

Other truths that are commonly missing are:
— celibacy is healthy
— persons of the opposite sex can be friends (they are real people, not just sex objects)
— sex is not love

— a responsible relationship is more satisfying than momentary bodily satisfaction

Pastors and mature Christians can promote the healing process by helping others to see truth on every level. Discussing belief systems with other Christians could be an important step toward health for the continuing playboys and playgirls.

Those using sex as only a temporary fix, such as immediately after a divorce or breakup, will quickly move into abstinence or relational sex. But those singles who continually need sex as a fix need the same kind of help that Christian alcoholics or gamblers need: knowledge of the truth, help in accepting responsibility for themselves, and a support group to help when they are tempted. Since sex has addicting elements, those who are using it as an escape or for other addictive reasons may need counseling or training to develop healthier behavior. Knowledge of the underlying motives for their sexual behavior might come from counseling. Some singles simply need training in the skills of friendship, the art of love, and the discipline of delayed gratification.

We all need the healing that comes from God. In our frayed state resulting from our misconceptions, as well as our deliberate rebellion and self-centeredness, we need the balm that comes from confession and the cleansing of forgiveness. Our pastors, elders, and mature Christian friends can administer this grace to us. Occasionally the bonding of sex becomes bondage—or the mind can be filled with bondage—and then we need the prayers of others for release.

Increasing numbers of Christian divorced and separated men and women are standing by their marriages, even when the spouse leaves, and not seeking release from their commitment. These plan to stay single and celibate until their spouses return. This focus on one marriage only can be very freeing in all other friendships because those standing by their marriages have declared themselves unavailable as spouses—only available as friends. To remain celibate is certainly a scriptural and healthy option, even if the ex-spouse does not return.

113

The apostle Paul says that those who do not seek marriage (or remarriage) are free from worldly cares and are more able to care for the Lord's wishes and seek how to please him (1 Cor. 7:32-35).

We need to examine our belief systems and seek the truth about our bodies, minds, emotions, and relationships. The more our internalized beliefs are in line with truth (reality), the more whole and joyful our living will be.

Celibates can be in need of healing, too, since all of our belief systems have error. Tamiko, although she had had a rich life of celibacy during her twenties, let some wrong beliefs get in the way of a peaceful life later on.

When Tamiko was thirty-three and desperately single, she sought the counsel of a very understanding pastor. He sympathized with her week after week as she struggled with her wretched singleness. Although her tears always flowed when she talked about God, the pastor felt so sorry she was single that it kept him from recognizing that singleness was not her problem. The real issue stemmed from her unwillingness to believe that God loved her and yet had not given her a spouse. She felt angry with her Creator because he wasn't providing what she wanted, and she felt rejected because she interpreted his lack of provision as lack of love. She had set up a role for him and the Almighty was not performing! God, not singleness, was her problem. Pastoral counseling for Tamiko needed to focus on her relationship with God first, reminding her that the God who had provided such rich relationships for her in the past was still alive and active in her life at thirty-three.

Singleness and Sex: A Summary

It seems apparent that a movement toward health is a movement away from casual sex. For those not yet contemplating abstinence, the direction to follow is to develop friendships, and to express oneself sexually in loving and caring relationships. Because of the potential for hurt, loving people generally move past the overlapping-lovers stage to a one-at-a-time position. As caring increases, most Christian singles find it inconsistent to express a total commitment in body and loyalty yet be unwilling to make a commitment to permanency in marriage. If marriage does not take place and the relationship breaks up, those singles moving toward health will generally have a time of abstinence; if an appropriate love-relationship develops they will then probably marry, and if no suitable mate appears they will probably continue to embrace the fullness of life and accept the gift of celibacy.

1. How can the church help establish belief systems in Christians that are in harmony with God's reality?

2. How can Christians influence public schools and the media to try to reveal more accurate truths about sex to the general population?

3. What are the most effective ways to help people who are damaging themselves by using sex other than in the way God intended?

4. What beliefs are necessary for singles if they are to choose celibacy?

7

A HEALTHY SINGLE IS A CHOOSER

*I*t is possible—not automatic, but possible—to be a whole and healthy celibate. Most of society does not look at singleness, especially celibate singleness, as healthy. The media today assume that anyone not sexually active is inadequate; but health comes not from sex, or even from marriage, but from several specific choices that singles can make. Health comes from taking charge of one's life rather than being a victim, from practicing agape-love rather than seeking sex, from developing friendships rather than just looking for lovers, from building a structure for one's time and relationships rather than passively waiting, and from developing one's uniqueness rather than seeking to be entertained. This chapter and the following chapters will detail how these objectives can be obtained.

Many singles feel like victims rather than choosers. We may feel rejected by a former spouse or by not being chosen at all. We may think we are victims of our heredity, our geography, or the timing of circumstances, not accepting that we can pick up from where we are at any time and choose the attitudes and life-styles we want. We are only victims if we choose to think that way, and we can influence our circumstances much more than we sometimes think.

Singles have more choices to make than those married, partly because fewer patterns and requirements are determined for singles, and partly because no one else is responsible for making choices for us. Therefore, recognizing that we are continually choosing, by action or by default, and learning to choose wisely are high priorities for a single.

117

Recognizing that Singleness Is a Choice

Knowing that one is single by choice is an essential ingredient for living a fulfilled single life. Few individuals have chosen to be permanently unwed, but some, especially women who have never been asked and men and women who are widowed or divorced against their wills, may say that they have had no choice. However, even though they may not have chosen to be single, anyone who has stayed unwed as an adult for over a couple of years is choosing singleness at this moment over any available option.

Some say, "But no one is available!" Not true. People are available somewhere since millions of unmarried persons roam this world, many looking for spouses. Singles who say that no one is available are implying either that those available are not desirable (which is a choice) or that living in the wrong place, being too busy, being afraid, or lack of knowledge prevent them from going where singles are available (another choice).

Some singles who find that all of those available around them are undesirable may not be getting to know these people. Our preconceived pictures of appropriate spouses may be the ones formed when we were sixteen and may now be inappropriate. Getting to know people in groups of similar interest can help in overcoming the prejudice that causes us to be rejecting.

Some singles focus on persons who do not reciprocate, again not being in tune with who they are, and not having changed their internal pictures appropriately. This is especially true of those who continue to choose persons too young. Older men could usually find many receptive women if they looked at people their own age.

The problem of not meeting people is a choice if singles choose to stay in places where no other singles live and choose not to use letters, dating services, contacts through relatives or friends, or vacation time to overcome geographic limitations.

Being too busy, being afraid, and lack of knowledge of where to meet people are all choices. Asking for help from those who have met with success and trying a variety of approaches add to the zest of living. But if we do not do anything about meeting possible mates, what is important to know is that we have made a choice, and a valid one. We can focus on other aspects of living for this period of time, and if at a future time we have more courage or more opportunity, or feel greater need, we can choose to change our patterns of living.

Most of us have postponed marriage for one of three reasons. We want to fulfill a goal before we marry, we want to wait for a better match than those that have been available so far, or we are afraid.

We hear singles making statements such as: "I'm not going to get involved with anyone until I finish school . . . pay off my loan . . . bury my bedridden mother . . . travel everywhere I want . . . establish myself in my career . . ." Postponing marriage for a goal is a choice, not an imperative, since other people in the same circumstances choose to marry. Postponing marriage is a valid choice; it is often the responsible choice, but it *is* a choice.

Those people waiting for a better match may think that they have had no chance to marry. This, also, is seldom true. They have chosen to stay single because their qualifications for a spouse were different from the criteria of those who married their rejects. Most of us eliminate as potential spouses great masses of people automatically by age, height, race, education, and religion before we even begin the personal checklists of humor, common interests, chemistry, and so forth. These standards are not necessarily bad, but we need to recognize that we are making a conscious choice to be single every time we refuse to date or to develop a relationship with someone who shows an interest in us.

So even those who have never been asked, or have been rejected, have still chosen to reject others, even in the embryo stages of friendship. Just look at the people who are married! Whatever the handicap a single feels is his or her cause of being rejected, someone with a greater handicap is married. We either choose to be unavailable or refuse to accept what is available.

Again, it is not wrong (and it can be wise) to have chosen to ignore those potential relationships; nor is it bad to be single. It is simply important that we be aware that we are choosing quality of life over marriage per se. Anyone for whom marriage is the primary goal can and will marry.

Armed with the knowledge that at this time we have chosen singleness and our own quality of life-style over indiscriminate marriage (marriage for the sake of marriage), we can examine how to expand that choosing ability in to healthy, fulfilled single living, whether temporarily or as a long-term life-style.

Knowing When to Stop Seeking a Spouse

Although marriage may be an appropriate goal for most singles in late adolescence and early adulthood, once that goal is attained most adults move on to achievement and self-actualization goals. Mature Christians concern themselves with ministry and the development and use of their gifts to become the unique creations God intended when he designed them.

Singles who delay marriage often feel that the goal of marriage must be reached before assuming full responsibility as adults. Marriage as a continual priority year after year often gives these men and women a desperate, grasping edge. Those whom the graspers see as potentials slide away as they see the grasping ones approach. This lockstep mentality of having to marry before broadening their view to see more of life also keeps these singles in a continual state of adolescence—not developing appropriate maturity, not developing loyalty or dependability or skills of friendship. Church people sometimes perpetuate the syndrome by thinking that the immaturity is owing to lack of marriage rather than to appropriate goals. Thus they continue to push marriage when goals of friendship and ministry might achieve maturity—and perhaps marriage, too—more quickly.

Those adults becoming single again may also get caught up in this intense priority of marriage. Singles' groups in

Southern California have a name for the syndrome of the continual seeker who goes from group to group looking for eligibles—the Singles' Shuffle. For a Single Shuffler, the major criterion for any activity is the probability of meeting "eligibles." The constant focus on marriage inhibits development of healthy, loyal friendships, and limits the effectiveness of these singles as contributing human beings growing into wholeness. Marriage as an option—being open to it but not actively seeking it—is quite different from marriage as a priority.

When a person is in school, or is recently healed from the trauma of divorce or widowhood, or has made a recent change of location or job that brings new people into view, then it may be appropriate to seek a spouse. These are times when people are most likely to be open to new relationships because of inner renewal or outer opportunities.

Those who are in routine patterns will do best for themselves, God, and marriage possibilities to pursue the development of their interests, talents, and service. In these pursuits the satisfaction of living and relationships will be found. Singles who are scolded by their marriage-conscious friends because they are too content, too busy, or have too many satisfying friendships to pursue marriage, perhaps do not need marriage at this time. Strangely, society has a way of making satisfied singles feel guilty, even when marriages are breaking up all around.

Ecclesiastes 3 (1-2, 5-6) tells us that "for everything there is a season, and a time for every matter under heaven: a time to be born, and a time to die; . . . a time to embrace, and a time to refrain from embracing; a time to seek, and a time to lose." Accordingly, in the rhythm of life, there is a time to seek a spouse and a time to refrain from seeking a spouse and to get on with living. Basically, we seek a spouse for our own comfort, to satisfy ourselves; therefore, the continuing search tends to make us self-centered. Giving ourselves space for a year or two to center on the more giving aspects of life, or even to build other relationships and elements of our lives, can be restful, fruitful, and a delight to the people whom we encounter regularly.

121

I would challenge anyone who has spent the past two years in The Search to take a two-year sabbatical. Imagine that for two years Mr. or Ms. Right is incommunicado at the South Pole without any way to meet you, and that you are therefore free to do whatever you want without the fear of missing out on the ideal mate. Freedom from the search is sometimes a great relief.

---

1. What choices do singles have about marriage when their dependent parents have to live with them and they have no time for dating?
2. Should you date or become better acquainted with people who do not meet your criteria for marriage?
3. What are the minimum requirements a person can have in seeking a spouse?
4. Why do people often become more attractive when they take a sabbatical from spouse-hunting?
5. Might a person miss the right mate by not being available?

Choosing a View of God

Another important choice we make is the decision of how we will view God. Because we have not followed the customary patterns of life, we may suddenly realize that God isn't fitting the image we had anticipated. The Creator is so much bigger than we can imagine, and has so many more dimensions than our minds can comprehend, that we do not need to get stuck with a limited view that damages us. Two elements that sometimes seem contradictory to us as singles are his sovereignty and his agape-love for us. If we accept his omnipotence without fully accepting our own responsibility, we may blame him for our singleness. If we believe that marriage is his gift to those he loves and singleness is his chastening of the undesirable, we can believe that we are not fully loved. Choosing to accept his love and sovereignty means asking him the hard questions and waiting for his answers.

The first point that we must discuss honestly with God is the question of sex. Although the Bible is very clear in telling us that we are loved, accepting God's love may not be easy if we accept his commandments too. If we believe that God expects abstinence of singles and also hold that sexual fulfillment is one of life's highest joys, yet God hasn't given us spouses, then how can we believe that God truly loves and understands us? Directly asking God our questions about sex is different from asking a friend, ourselves, or the wind, yet discussing our sex lives, our fantasies, and our desires with the One who made us and loves us is essential for healthy growth.

Marriage is the other issue we must settle with God if we are to fully accept his love for us in our single state. If marriage seems like God's best plan, and he seems to be denying that gift to us, then direct encounter with him on that subject is fundamental to the healing of that fear, that doubt of his love and power. He can change our perspectives so that we see life in a broader scope than the typical lockstep time sequence that seems normal to us. The Bible is full of situations where God uses timing that seems delayed to the humans he is working with: Abraham and Sarah past the age of ninety at the birth of the promised son, Moses beginning his life work at eighty, and Hannah waiting so long for Samuel, for examples.

To be healthy, a person must be undergirded by love, and only God's love is deep enough and unselfish enough to provide that sure footing for our ability to be what he created us to be. Accepting God's total love for us—as his creation, his redeemed, placed into his own body, made heirs with him for eternity—accepting this love forms a basis for our self-acceptance as worthy persons, worthy friends, and worthy contributors to God's kingdom wherever our lot may fall. The love is available, we must *choose* to accept it.

Now, wrapped in this love, we can be further assured of our place in God's purpose by being reminded of his flawless ability to plan what he wants and to pull it off. Isaiah's prophecies remind us of Jehovah's power when Isaiah foretells exactly what God is going to do to each king and nation and then he does it. God's purpose in Joseph's life, as Joseph explained to his brothers in Genesis 50:20, is another example of the careful planning of God, even though understood by Joseph only in hindsight: "As for you, you meant evil against me; but God meant it for good, to bring it about that many people should be kept alive, as they are today." If we wipe out of our minds that marriage is the only good plan—the best plan—and let our lives be full of joy each day, we will be free to experience the fullness of God's purposes for us. In brief, we can *choose* to trust that he has plans for our good and that he is capable of fulfilling them.

Choosing to Be Responsible for Oneself

Unless singles take care of their own basic needs and comforts, they are in no position to reach out to others in love—only in need. Much spouse-seeking involves inadequate people desperately trying to find others to take care of them. To be a healthy married or a healthy single requires accepting responsibility for oneself. Therefore, another important prerequisite for health is to view oneself as responsible and to see oneself accurately from God's perspective.

When we view ourselves as eternal beings, sons and daughters of the Creator, and destined to be joint rulers with the Ruler of the universe, it doesn't matter much whether we are married or single, parents or childless, career successes or unemployed. The essential fact is that we are unduplicated beings created for unique relationships and purposes, and, though we are fallible and do not live up to our high calling, we are forgiven.

Since our images of ourselves determine our behavior, seeing ourselves as capable and responsible is essential. When those married are inadequate, the caring of the spouse may compensate for their helplessness; but singles are more vulnerable, since no one is there to cover for them. Therefore, healthy singles must train their minds to accept the capable sides of themselves, realistically acknowledging limitations, of course, but focusing on all the abilities that God has given us.

Our self-image is based on statements we have mentally accepted about ourselves. The more we dwell upon our capabilities rather than our failures, our potential rather than our limitations, our accomplishments rather than our fiascos, the more we will operate as worthwhile beings. We are responsible for the words we use about ourselves inside our heads because these words determine our expectations of ourselves, and therefore our productivity.

If the concept of singleness is negative to some unmarried persons, they are limiting their potential. Accepting the time of singleness as a gift for growth, adventure, and freedom to love, give, and build puts the emphasis on living rather than on waiting or grasping.

---

1. How do we know if God's best for us is singleness?
2. Is God responsible for our singleness, or are we?
3. If because of our own deliberate sin we miss some good God may desire for us, can we repent and still have a life blessed by God? (Remember the prodigal son, Luke 15:11-32.)
4. What positive statements about singleness, your life, or yourself can you make that will enhance your self-image and your image of singleness?

Aloneness, Solitude, Contemplation—Not Loneliness

Loneliness is not caused by singleness, but rather by a mindset that says, Someone ought to be here. Right after someone leaves—a spouse, a child, a friend—it is natural to miss that person's presence for a time, but the lonely feeling diminishes daily. However, a generalized loneliness—missing a fantasized or unknown somebody—is irresponsible, bordering on self-pity. Loneliness, like sex, is in the mind. Each of us has the responsibility to reach out to others in love, to establish our own community, and to learn to enjoy our own company; single or married, these are the disciplines of any mature person. Imagining that someone else is responsible or that one's need can be met by one person—spouse or friend—stunts the fearful person and usually drowns any relationship that the person attempts. Taking responsibility to establish time with people and to enjoy time alone is essential for healthy living.

Aloneness is marvelous. As singles we can choose to be alone, or choose to be with the particular people we want. Because we have the freedom to order our leisure time, we can develop our unique potential. The idea-person is free to think, meditate, write, pray, do research, read. The visual or object-oriented person has the option to design, build, paint, travel, photograph, do crafts. The people-person has opportunity to listen, communicate, host dinners, attend parties, visit the sick and elderly, sponsor a little brother or sister, or adopt a foster child. The scope of possibilities is endless if a person chooses to order time responsibly rather than to wallow in the marsh of loneliness.

The greatest difficulty with these options is that they take initiative, and initiative takes energy, and when we are down, our energy has oozed all over the floor. At this point one is very vulnerable to attacks of loneliness and depression. The old saying, "Never make a decision after sundown," emphasizes the effect tiredness has on our emotions. Unless we have built a routine into our lives that can carry us through these times and know how to comfort ourselves, we may take a tailspin into self-pity.

Comfort

The starting point is comfort. When we are tired and lonely what we want is someone else to take the initiative. Even pursuing interests that we normally enjoy can seem to require insurmountable effort when our minds are spiraling downward toward loneliness, self-pity, and depression. Again, our minds are the keys. We can allow ourselves to dwell on loneliness and destructive thoughts or actions, or we can comfort ourselves constructively (or at least less destructively).

Our primary comfort areas are mouth and genitals as we search for sensual gratification. When a child is fearful, unhappy, or uncertain he may grab for his penis or put a thumb in his mouth. As adults, these actions convert to masturbation, smoking, eating, drinking, and sometimes nail-biting and thumbsucking.

Masturbation used as a relief when thought or sight has suddenly aroused the body may be the fastest way to bring the mind back to a productive focus. Fighting the desire to masturbate when the body is aroused may take all evening and waste much more time than getting it over with. However, masturbation as a comfort—that is, deliberately seeking fantasies that make climax possible—may be an acceptable means of comfort at some stage of growth but may also be harmful, depending on the fantasy. Since vivid imagination acts on our brains as though we had had the experience, and what we experience becomes part of our memory system, it is important not to visualize persons we know or real situations because we tend to act in real life as though our fantasy has actually happened. Most of us have had the experience of someone behaving inappropriately toward us, assuming rights not in character with the reality of the relationship. Usually the imaginations of these people have been working overtime. What we do with our minds determines how we live.

Both men and women celibates can go for long periods of time without masturbation if the mind is set on nonsexual things (things above, the apostle Paul would say). When men have been sexually active, their bodies may need to be relieved at first; but, after a period of celibacy, there seems to be no physical need for masturbation if the mind is celibate.

Since the Bible does not mention masturbation and Bible writers had no shyness about enumerating sexual sins, I see masturbation as a possible halfway house. For adolescents, masturbation is a way to learn control of the body. For engaged women, fantasy about their fiancés probably helps prepare them for sexual intercourse in marriage. For mature marrieds or singles, it may be used when necessary for relief, and occasionally for comfort. As our minds grow to think God's thoughts we need masturbation less. The drop-off is gradual and natural for most singles who are seeking to grow toward healthiness.

Other popular comforts are food, drink, and shopping. Most of us when we are restless or lonely have to fight the temptation to indulge our mouths with our favorite taste treat. We can, however, learn to reward or comfort ourselves with a favorite food or drink if we practice seeing ourselves as responsible, worthwhile people who do not need to gorge. Likewise with shopping, getting out among people in a store can lift the spirits, and great discipline is necessary only if one is a credit card addict.

A valuable activity is to think through the safe comforts in which we might indulge ourselves when we are too tired or downhearted to be productive and are tempted to put negative thoughts into our heads. Luxurious baths, physical exercise, puttering, reading, music, and television can all block from the mind those negatives that undermine productivity and peace. Since sleep is the great healer, it will probably suffice to find a comfort to encourage sleepiness. Once sleep has healed, the morning mindset will make possible a fresh start.

For people with recurring bouts of loneliness, restlessness, or excessive escapism, some lists may also be helpful. Make a list of wants—things you want to do that can be done alone, especially activities that are available on evenings, Sundays, or whenever your attacks occur. Wants give energy, so if you look at your list before the energy level drops too low, you can probably reverse the downtrend and become involved in an activity that not only takes your mind off loneliness, but also makes you feel worthwhile—and begins to change your mindset.

The other list comprises comforts, those items that make you feel you are caring for yourself rather than being destructive. Physical comforts such as a hot tub, a facial, a bubble bath, or curling up by the fire can help you feel worthwhile if you program the words inside your head to say so. Visual comforts like art books, hummingbirds, the colors of a leaf, or old trip slides can rest the mind. Active comforts like a drive, gardening, or shooting baskets can alleviate restlessness, since exercise often increases the energy level. The comfort list is to be used when the level of motivation is too low to accomplish the more mundane activities, like cleaning out the closet or organizing the slide file. The lists can be helpful because when the mind becomes stuck on a habitual idea like loneliness, it sometimes blanks out the creative thoughts that are available to you when your energy is flowing.

Some people find Scripture helpful at these times, while those who have a praise language may be able to use this to block destructive thoughts and move again with positive energy. However, when some people's thoughts are negatively colored, their impressions of God become warped also, so taking one's thoughts too seriously at times of loneliness is unwise. It is better to blank one's mind until an accurate mental filter is in place again.

Choosers

All humans live more fully if they are aware of their power of choice. However, since singles have no one legitimate to lean on except God, and their pathways are not clearly marked, they have an even greater need than married persons to develop their abilities to choose. The freedom of singleness is far greater, but so is the responsibility.

---

1. What is the difference between loneliness and aloneness?
2. In what ways might masturbation be wrong? Or helpful?
3. What comforts best compensate for sex?
4. How can lists of wants and comforts help a person be a chooser instead of a victim?

8

A HEALTHY SINGLE PRACTICES LOVING

Singles may have a tendency to be self-centered since they often have obligations to no one but themselves. Two aspects of selfishness that are common tendencies of the unmarried are self-pity and self-indulgence. Choosing to take responsibility for ourselves decreases the probability of self-pity, and recognizing that love is God's purpose for us, instead of focusing on our own comforts and needs, helps move us outward.

For the sake of simplicity, we will use the term *love* in this chapter to refer to agape (disregarding, for the moment, other varieties of love such as eros). Scripture presents agape-love as the quality God desires of all human beings. Jesus specifies this kind of love when he speaks of the primary job God has given people to do here on earth: "You shall love the Lord your God with all your heart, and with all your soul, and with all your mind. This is the great and first commandment. And a second is like it, You shall love your neighbor as yourself" (Matt. 22:37, 38). Having chosen to accept God's love for us, we naturally respond by loving him and wanting to get on with his purpose for our lives. His purpose for us is to learn to love.

Although God's general method of teaching humans the principles of agape-love is through the hardships of marriage and raising a family, he expects singles to be involved with people so that we, too, may learn the art of loving. The single must take initiative to be in and stay in relationships with people in order for God to teach him or her to love. The single person can escape the sandpaper of closeness that may rub us the wrong way more easily than the married person can escape it. Staying involved and vulnerable is a major discipline for the single.

How Love Acts

So how does this love work, and how does it relate to sex? The first requisite is that we practice this love on everyone we meet—"our neighbors": men and women, people at work and at social events, young and old, "eligibles" and "ineligibles." If we are not experienced in loving, we do not have the skills to form a good marriage or a good friendship.

Many elements of love or friendship could be listed, but Paul's list in Colossians 3:12, 13 forms a good base for understanding this purpose of God for us. Using the image of clothing oneself for business, Paul specifies a list of qualities that we are to "put on" and then says, "And over all these virtues put on love, which binds them all together in perfect unity" (v. 14 NIV). In other words, love is the outer garment that contains the others and orders them for activity.

Listen to Paul's list of love's virtues (some of which fit his description of love in 1 Corinthians 13:4-8): compassion (empathy), kindness, lowliness (humbleness of mind), meekness (gentleness), patience, forbearing one another, and forgiving one another. Paul draws a surprising contrast in this chapter between what he tells us to put to death and what he tells us to put on. "Put to death therefore," he says in verse 5, "what is earthly in you" and begins his list with sexual sins: fornication (immorality), impurity, passion, evil desire, and covetousness. When he contrasts sexual sins with their opposite—what we are to put on—he does not begin with chastity or abstinence, but rather with compassion and kindness, elements of a truly loving person.

Loving in this way makes us vulnerable because we extend ourselves by being attentive, caring, taking time, and even risking being put down or used. It especially takes our time, and time is one of the real advantages to singleness. This kind of love also does not promise any immediate return on the investment, such as marriage, popularity, fun, or job advancement. It is noticing the persons closest and responding to them as important human beings—quite different from the immediate satisfaction we expect from sex.

Empathy does not require the development of a deep friendship, or even necessarily the sharing of oneself or a commitment to the future; empathy asks a personal awareness of and caring for each person who comes into our lives. Empathy means looking at people and really seeing them, listening to a person and hearing with understanding, and feeling the emotion that is behind the words or look. Empathy or compassion is "feeling with" our neighbor so that he or she, young or old, quick or slow, feels heard. We love with our eyes by looking into the eyes of others, with our mouths by being silent while we listen, with our ears by waiting for answers to our questions that indicate our interest, by our words, which show acceptance without judgment. Empathy is listening with care.

Kindness is acting in a way that shows consideration for others' needs. As it takes time to listen carefully, so it takes time to offer help, to give a ride, to make a salad, to help clean up, to change a tire, or put up a shelf. Many times we singles look to our married friends for exchanges of help because they may seem more available or stable, but singles need to be aware of other singles who need help, too, especially those who are away from their families and relatives.

Humbleness of mind is the refusal to consider oneself better than all of those other old singles out there in that drab-looking singles' group. We all hate to be categorized into whatever pigeonhole has a negative connotation for us: old, single, red-necked, uppity—whatever names frighten us. We are afraid of being identified with people we think are not "our kind of people," or of being trapped with persons who might bore us, and we are afraid of being misunderstood—perhaps as seeking romance when all we want is to be friendly. As singles we sometimes feel more secure arriving somewhere with a date who is "our kind of person" so that our identity is secured, since alone we are much more vulnerable socially. Loving everyone is a real risk to singles—risk of time, of possible embarrassment, of getting uncomfortably trapped—but this is how we grow. What God is calling us to do if we are to be healthy, happy humans is to accept everyone else as our equals.

Gentleness and *patience* are characteristics that are particularly well learned in raising children. Where is this learned by the single who has not battled through the daily grind of whining voices and unreasonable demands? The sanctuary of our homes is one of the joys of singleness, but if we are to mature as healthy individuals, to truly learn to love, we need to expose ourselves to demanding people. This can be in service to children, to the sick, to the elderly—somewhere where our potential for gentleness and patience must be tested.

In my naiveté as a young college graduate, I was under the misconception that I did not have a temper. I had been about thirteen when my last outburst of anger had occurred, except for a few pithy words to my father on occasion, which I didn't count. Teaching fifth grade totally disillusioned me about my patience and calmness; I had no idea that I could become so angry! Children will bring it out—especially children *en masse* or with an opposing objective. Gentleness and patience are learned in situations where wills clash.

Forbearing one another is another quality that may be more easily developed in marriage because every spouse has some characteristic that is irritating. We singles can escape if we choose and lose out on the growth in agape-love. To practice forbearance and love, we can hang in with the singles' group and all its peculiarities rather than escaping by trying to find a group that seems more appealing. It may be long-term friends, persons at work, or members of some interest group that provide opportunity to practice forbearance. Practice is available everywhere if we can resist the temptation to run off.

Forgiving one another is one of the most basic elements of mental health. Some singles are still blaming ex-spouses for leaving or dying, while others are blaming parents for molding them into unmarriageable creatures. We blame bosses, neighbors, teachers, pastors, and other individuals for making our lives what they are. Even if we take responsibility to go on with our lives, sometimes we still hang on to past injustices. Lack of forgiveness is a cancer that eats at us, tensing our bodies, tightening our jaws, and even making our eyes cold. We limit our ability to love people—even people not involved in the injustice—if we cling to this cold rock of unforgiveness. Being forgiven is tied with our ability to forgive in the Lord's model prayer: "Forgive us our debts, *as* we also have forgiven our debtors" (Matt. 6:12). Again and again in Scripture God claims the exclusive right of vengeance: "Vengeance is mine, I will repay," says the Lord (Rom. 12:19; *see also* Ps. 94:1). Our lack of forgiveness may make the object of our unforgiveness uncomfortable, but that damage is minuscule compared to the damage it does to us. If any lump of unforgiveness still remains from past marriages or hurts, settling it alone or with pastoral or psychological help is essential for health.

---

1. Who are the nonperfect people God has given you to love in order to test your patience, forbearance, humility, empathy, and other qualities of love?
2. Which of the qualities of love listed on pages 131–34 do you find most difficult to practice?

Can Dating Be Loving?

Our expectations sometimes make dating an unloving process. Anyone who has had longtime friendships or good relationships with relatives has developed some characteristics of agape-love, but selfish expectations of a date may cause us to set aside love while we evaluate the candidate. Traditional dating in our society has a strong connotation of using people, which is emphasized by our automatic checklists. Does his car measure up? Are her clothes classy? How much does he tip? Does she expect me to pay for everything? What is his occupation? How would she fit with my friends? Does he believe in women's rights? Can she cook? The lists vary, but the candidating concept remains. Is this love?

We expect a large chunk of our emotional needs to be met by a lover, while we usually are more reasonable with friends. Selfish eros dominates in most singles' circles when we discuss dating. "After all," we say, "why continue a relationship if my needs are not being met? There must be someone out there who can meet my needs." And there may be—in the first flush of a new eros. Union again appeases loneliness, new stimulus reawakens pleasure, until one takes a deep breath above the merging and recognizes again the individuality of the partner, and the essential aloneness of one's being.

Expectations become even more confused when singles become older—even as to whether both persons think of each other as eligible marriage partners, or simply as business acquaintances or Christian siblings. Friendships between men and women extend through all ages, races, and socioeconomic backgrounds—more varieties of people than would be comfortable in marriage. Since comfort is enhanced by knowing the ground rules, it sometimes helps to make some general statement about the friendship that can cue the other person. The expectation of friendship or simply enjoying another's company in a loving and giving way is certainly healthier than labeling every man-woman activity as a "date" with all of the expectations of a potential spouse.

Many times explicitly stating one's expectations is best. For example, a divorcée was excited about the new widower in her life but was puzzled by his alternating hot and cold behavior. Finally, they had a frank discussion about their friendship when he explained that to him she wasn't "eligible" since he didn't plan to marry someone divorced. She accepted his position, and they became comfortable friends since the boundaries of the relationship were defined.

To be loving at this stage of relating between men and women is to regard the other person as someone with worth, with feelings, and with the need to know what your expectations are. Embarrassment can cause a person to communicate too abruptly and hurt the other person, or it can keep a person from communicating at all and leave the other standing without knowing what happened. Humbleness

135

of mind—that is, not thinking of oneself as better than the other—encourages one to communicate clearly and kindly.

A common expectation of dating in the secular world that carries over into Christian circles is that dating is using—financially, socially, or sexually. Women say, "I don't particularly care for the guy, but at least I will see that play I've been wanting to see." Meanwhile men say, "She cooks well, so I'll get a good dinner out of the evening anyway." We can use dates as entries to social situations, or for physical pleasure to satisfy our bodies. None of these kinds of dating is loving. Compassion (empathy), the first requirement of being a loving person, requires that we regard each other with care, concerned about our "neighbor's" needs.

Dating and the Sex Question

Dating with agape-love means that we must learn to say no to casual sex, since sexual intercourse without commitment is not a loving act. In any relationship between possible "eligibles" the question of what to do about sex must be settled in order for them to be comfortable. Knowing each other's expectations in this crucial area alleviates some of the uncomfortable game-playing. Nonverbal communication may be sufficient, but most people are more comfortable if expectations and reasons are eventually clarified.

Recently divorced men who haven't dated for the past decade or two have been shocked to find a seemingly "nice" woman taking the initiative to suggest going to bed. Some men have the ability to laugh their way through those conversations, smoothly turning the talk in a different direction so that it seems the suggestion was never made. Other men who may not feel ready for this kind of involvement are pushed by the macho-male image to perform, and often become emotionally hooked. Talking about sex directly is becoming more and more necessary because we have such different experiences and expectations. Men now need to learn how to say no and to discern their own feelings in situations where women initiate.

For the abstainer, going through the conversation with

date after date to find out if the partner is willing to continue dating without genital involvement can become very tiring. One woman stated, "I won't date anyone again who doesn't first know me as a person." Another woman sighed, "I wish I could carry a tape recorder with me on the first few dates so that, when the inevitable questions come up, I could simply flip on my tape and say, 'Here's my answer.' "

Dating new people becomes boring for most singles because it is repetitive, an endless cycle of the same old questions with each new date, and because the relating is only shallow unless the relationship lasts. Most continuing singles who are not stuck on the have-to-marry carrousel form a variety of friends for different occasions with perhaps one or two special friends whom they see more frequently.

For singles who are eligible for each other and continue to date but choose to abstain from sex, the mating instinct may initially be very high, but usually diminishes as personal intimacy grows. The need to take care of and truly love the other person becomes a higher desire than satisfying one's own body. Not that the sexual desire dies—couples must still set and maintain habits with each other that protect them from being irresponsible toward each other—but the depth of responsible love delays sex until the appropriate time. Practicing love means getting to know one's own bodily responses and limits. Walking this tightrope lovingly probably means sometimes being too hot, sometimes too cold—a continual process of learning and deciding. For Christians, one of the fruits of the Spirit who dwells in us is self-discipline, so we are not left helpless.

As a dating friendship continues, we are even more obligated to practice the art of love. Reviewing the apostle Paul's virtues of agape-love in relation to dating provides some more clues as to how we can be truly healthy singles.

Dating with Empathy

Compassion, empathy, or feeling with another person is demonstrated by listening to the feelings that a person is communicating. People do not usually share meaningfully

137

unless they trust, however, and unless the other person shares equally—which means that the partner who shares least determines the depth of any friendship. When one shares deeply and the other mainly listens without reciprocating later, it's not a friendship or partnership, it's therapy. The listener is taking the role of counselor, pastor, or parent, which is most unhealthful in a relationship that is supposed to be a friendship.

So how do we trust a date? Some people are riskers and share themselves easily—or seem to, since we all keep some secrets. Others find something in the other person on which to base trust such as reputation, the vibes they feel, or the way the person listens. For most people, building trust takes time together in relaxed circumstances where conversations can flow easily. Some people are so busy talking or doing that they do not allow for time to communicate feelings.

A woman described three dates with a man she was hoping to get to know but finally gave up on. The first date was dinner—good chance to talk, she thought, except that he brought along another couple and the two men talked continually about work, so the two women became acquainted. Next was the ball game—at least there would be time to talk between plays or innings, she hoped, but he kept himself busy elbowing for hotdogs and figuring percentages at every break. Fighting traffic to and from the game did not even allow for relaxed conversation in the car. The third date was similar. Every possible moment of time for exploratory conversation was cut off by busy-ness, loud music, or other people. She gave up, and he probably had no idea that his providing entertainment for her missed the point of relationship.

Dating with Kindness

Paul's second virtue of love—kindness—focuses one's attention on the other person. In dating, people are usually concerned about impressing the other person or having their own needs met. To act kindly toward others means to focus on them enough to know what they like, want, or feel in order to find something kind to do for them. Some people, however, check out other people's wants and do favors for them in order to manipulate something in return. These acts produce guilt and anger in the manipulated, but a genuine act of kindness sends off vibes of caring.

Being kind on a date is not insisting on your own way, although you should express your wants and likes, and not leave all responsibility for having a good time on one partner. Unkind is the person who sits back, imperially waiting to judge the entertainment.

Kindness comes in little acts of thoughtfulness, a sincere compliment, jumping up to get something the other wants, and remembering things that will please. Kindness is not keeping score as in, "I paid this time. She pays next." It is not comparing gifts as in, "I got him a thirty-dollar shirt, and he only sent me a potholder." When we give, we must forget our own act of kindness, or else it isn't love, it is manipulation. Some of us have a hard time giving without counting the return, an evidence that we have not yet fully accepted the bigness of God's love for us.

Dating with Humbleness

Third on Paul's list of ways to love is humbleness of mind—not thinking too highly of ourselves. It is boring to date a braggart. Some men feel that they must impress their dates with how important they are: their job, their car, their possessions, or their intelligence. Women often show lack of humility (and a lack of security!) by referring to brand names, putting down other women who don't have class, or letting it be known that they only go to the best restaurants, order exquisite cuisine, and expect royal attendance on them at all times. Any show of this attitude of superiority can inhibit a man's spontaneity to suggest, "Let's grab a hamburger and walk through the park!" One person's intellectual snobbery can prevent the other from sharing a great thought taken out of the *Reader's Digest*. The financial expectations of a woman can certainly increase a man's feeling of being used.

Feeling or acting superior is not love: love is feeling

genuine equality of worth with everyone. Certainly we are different, since some are smarter or richer or have greater expertise than others. But love does not compare; it brings out the best in whatever the date has to offer.

Dating with Gentleness and Patience

Developing a friendship takes time. Women, especially, tend to become demanding if progress toward marriage is not made according to their timetables, whereas men sometimes push the sex issue. Gentleness, Paul's fourth item, is not demanding.

In helping the growth of a friendship, patience is needed since each of us has our own way of developing trust. To push impatiently, to demand too soon, to expect the friendship to follow our preconceived patterns is not love. Love is patient.

Forbearing One Another in Dating

In every friendship there are peculiarities of the other person that we need to bear with: the lost keys, checking the lock twice, picking at lint, or clearing the throat. As a friendship progresses we are bound to find little peculiarities that are difficult to change and not worth making into big issues. Love accepts these traits with tenderness, as an integral part of the person loved, something to overlook or shrug a shoulder at in acceptance. Love is forbearing.

Dating with Forgiveness

Last on the list of Paul's virtues of love is forgiveness. A friendship hasn't passed into depth if nothing has happened that needs forgiving. In any intimate relationship, particularly between a man and a woman, wrongs are committed. They are often unintentional, but they hurt nevertheless.

During a friendship of several years, Tamiko thought she had adjusted to her friend's habit of being late, but one Sunday became a crucial test. For more than an hour she had been standing in the sun, sweltering in a hot church suit with her stomach clamoring for the lunch he had invited her to share. Then one of his neighbors told Tamiko that fifteen minutes before she had come he had left to look at a car with his brother. Angrily she stormed home knowing of no excuse for his thoughtlessness. She waited for his phone call knowing that this was the end of their friendship because she could not possibly let herself be vulnerable again to one who cared so little for her feelings. When the phone rang, she poured out her accusations as he listened. He explained, saying he had hoped he would be back in time, and admitted that he had made the wrong choice and was sorry. The silence lengthened as Tamiko realized that she could now say good-bye or forgive. "Come over," she said, and they began again, on a new level now, because they had safely crossed an incident of hurt with forgiveness.

Learning to love puts us in the mainstream of God's purpose for our lives. Extending that love to all of our "neighbors," not just focusing on those persons we think are going to meet our needs, is one aspect of being healthy. Operating with God's kind of love in our dating and male-female friendships strengthens our health and happiness.

However, "going it alone"—trying to be loving in all situations without building some reciprocal friendships—is not practical and is not God's plan for us. We need to be loved back. As singles, we are responsible for building a base of friendships that provide us with love so that we can love those who cannot love back.

1. How is dating with agape-love different from the usual American adult kind of dating?
2. What happens if one person loves with true giving and the other takes advantage?
3. Is there a time to stop loving?

9

A HEALTHY SINGLE
IS A FRIEND

Not all singles can build friendships with the opposite sex. Those who view the other sex as sex objects, rather than persons, cannot be friends. However, those who will discipline their minds to view and women as people to know and enjoy, rather than objects to meet their needs—sex or marriage—can build a rich and satisfying life of friendships.

The chart on page 141 indicates five kinds of love and friendship people can enjoy. Agape, the choosing-to-do-good-for-another kind of love God commands us to give, we have discussed in chapters 1 and 8. Eros, the selfish, exciting, limiting, and fantastically absorbing desire for merger, was defined in chapter 1. In this chapter we will discuss three additional kinds of love, which we call friendship: companionship, mind-friend, and soul-mate or intimate, as well as the need for male-female friendships.

A marriage is usually initiated by eros, stabilized and continued by companionship, and made enduring by agape, the will to care for the spouse. Some marriage partners are mind-friends, but this is not essential; and those able to trust can become soul-mates and have personal intimacy along with the physical intimacy of marriage, but many marriages survive without the sharing of souls. So if the essentials of marriage are companionship and agape with a little eros thrown in for spice, ordinary friendships can have only one dimension and be satisfactory.

Since singles have the option of choosing different people to enjoy as friends, knowing the characteristics of companion, mind-friend, and soul-mate helps us not to expect too

CHARACTERISTICS OF FRIENDSHIPS

Type of Love	Based On	Involvement ↓Effect	Characteristics	Where to Meet	Communication	Length
Romantic "Eros" Lover	Body chemistry, physical attraction.	Body ↓merging	Intense, exclusive, possessive, limited age, race, male/female.	Social settings, church, school introductions.	Topics: Each other, the relationship. Face to Face. Focus on each other.	Maximum thirty months if mutual and fulfilled. Indefinite if fantasy.
Companionship "Storge"	Availability, familiarity.	Affection ↓comfort	Casual, nonexclusive, nonpossessive, any age, race, male/female, even pets.	Family, work, neighborhood, church, school, interest groups.	Topics: trivia, happenings, gossip, Side by Side. Focus Outward.	As long as paths conveniently cross.
Mind-Friend "Philia" Friendship	Mind chemistry, common intellectual interests.	Mind ↓creativity	Similar intellect, any race, sex, marital status.	School, work, boards, projects, think tanks.	Topics: Ideas, concepts, plans, problem-solving. Side by Side.	Permanent. Can usually be picked up after a long absence.
Soul-mate Intimacy Spiritual Friend	Mutual trust, desire to share.	Emotion ↓intimacy	Exclusive, but not possessive Can be male/female any race or age.	Church, family, conferences, work, travel partners.	Topics: feelings, personal growth, God, prayer, meaning, Face to Face.	Permanent. Can be picked up after a long absence.
Goodwill "Agape"	The will, God's command.	Will ↓kindness	Choose to do good for others. Unaffected by race, sex, age.	Everywhere.	Acts and words of kindness, honesty, and affirmation.	Whenever people are present or thought of.

much from one person. Many people would make good companions, yet have no mind-click with us at all. Some soul-mates are so intense that once a week is all that the soul can take, and it becomes a relief simply to have a companion to saunter along with. Sometimes we reject giving people even a small place in our lives because they do not live up to some arbitrary checklist, even when we are not looking for a mate; but we can find much joy and stability in a variety of friends who touch only small portions of our lives.

The idea of friendship without eros is very appealing to people at certain stages of their lives. An attractive young man in a seminar voiced a familiar complaint: "I would love to have a woman friend right now. After distancing myself from women for ten years because of a bad marriage, I finally fell in love again six months ago, but she left me after a few months. Although I'm not ready for another romantic relationship, I need a friend, but when I walk into the singles' group at church, it's electric. I wouldn't dare try to be friends with anyone there—they would immediately think romance." How true and how sad that a young man needing caring friendship would only be identified as a wonderful prospect, a sex object, in a young singles' group. Generally, places specifically identified "for singles" breed a mating mentality. It is rare to be free enough from the romantic illusion in such a group to be able to form companions or mind-friends, for eros is usually the object. There are some groups however in which nonromantic friendships can emerge because they have a strong enough core of men and women who truly care for each other as friends and who focus on group activities.

As the chart on page 143 shows, characteristics of companions, mind-friends, and soul-mates are quite different from characteristics of eros. When our minds can clearly see that nonerotic friendships have an important place in our lives, and when the elements of such friendships are clarified, singles will be freer to pursue companions, mind-friends, and soul-mates.

Companionship

C. S. Lewis uses the Greek word *storge* to identify the kind of affection we feel for familiar creatures: the dog, the children, the gardener, or even the spouse. This kind of affection characterizes companionship. Companionship is based primarily on availability. Its purposes are to comfort, to alleviate loneliness, to keep the wheels of humanness—agape-love—oiled, and to develop affection. Companionship is nonexclusive—that brotherly, family affection that isn't focused on the other person, just pleasure and ease in being together.

Although a stranger can be a momentary companion, for example, in a class, on a trip, or in a pub, availability is usually determined by those familiar creatures around us. The available people can be any age, either sex, any race or faith as long as they are willing to be in one's company. Presence is the main feature of companionship, just somebody to be around, somebody comfortable who makes little demand.

Companionship can be a dilemma for people living alone. Where do you find the person to go shopping with or to chat with over coffee? Who will make appreciative clucks over your latest purchase or victory with the boss? And who will sympathize with the leak in your car's radiator?

Singles have solved the need for companionship in many ways. Jerry's wife left him with a four-bedroom house, a fourteen-year-old son, and a large dog when she divorced him. Being used to much activity around the house, Jerry immediately rented both spare rooms to young men who had been friends of his married son. The activity around the house eased the pain of divorce and provided new interests as each person shared his culinary skills, car problems, and girlfriend frustrations with the rest of the household.

Some have roommates, neighbors, or relatives who are available for spontaneous socializing or company while eating, shopping, or going to a movie, but most singles need to plan regular social activities in order to keep balanced. Scheduled activities such as volleyball, hiking, Bible studies, and classes are especially helpful to someone new in a locality or newly single, as well as being a meeting place for friends.

Gwen, working long hours to establish her own dress shop, was "adopted" by a nearby family where she was welcome to drop in for a chat with the adults and to play "auntie" to the kids. She became fast friends with the three-year-old boy, enjoying their outings more and more as he became school-aged. Parks, mountain streams, the beach, even exploring markets and downtown buildings became adventures when she shared these forays with a growing boy.

Leonard became a Big Brother to a ten-year-old boy, indulging his own enjoyment of sports while satisfying his need to do something worthwhile. He still sees his "little brother" occasionally even though the "boy" is now in his twenties.

Jean lives a block from Myrtle, a retired school teacher from her school district. As Myrtle's money and energy for traveling have decreased, Jean has found Myrtle a companion with whom to go shopping, to take in a movie, to test a new recipe, or to watch the cat when Jean is out of town. Myrtle is genuinely interested in Jean's work, her home, and her family, whom Myrtle has met over the years. Since Myrtle is usually available, Jean has the pleasure of a ready listener and companion without having to program these activities into her already busy schedule.

Fortunately, Myrtle has not become dependent on Jean as her sole or primary companion, since Jean's work and family take a big chunk of her time, while Myrtle, being retired, has more leisure. Myrtle is active in a number of clubs and classes as well as being an expert gardener. The problems of one-sided companionships that put uncomfortable demands on the busier person sometimes scare people into not reaching out, but being explicit about limits to the relationship can keep both persons comfortable and relating.

Eileen talked several of her coworkers into joining the same health club. Not only did this provide a regular time for chatting with people she wanted to be with, but also after a few months she had established a number of acquaintances with whom she could share groans in aerobics and casual talk in the spa. Having a neutral place to meet such as a gym, class, restaurant, or church activity, can provide casual

146

companionship without the stress of hosting or continued initiating.

Some singles are fortunate in having members of their family living nearby whom they enjoy. Celeste's favorite younger brother lived just twenty miles away with his wife, whom Celeste also liked. They planned dinner together at least every other week. Her brother was willing to help Celeste with repair jobs around her house, and Celeste was available for baby-sitting when her nephew arrived. Marian's bachelor cousin, who lived across town, was usually available when Marian needed an extra man for a dinner party. Marian's gourmet cooking made her invitations most welcome. JoAnne and her widowed mother rented apartments in the same building. They shared rides, traded off jobs around their apartments, and even shared a cat, who roamed back and forth to whichever owner was home. This arrangement allowed independence, but help in times of need.

Sometimes companionship can be combined with being helpful to someone else, such as adopting a family with small children needing baby-sitting, becoming a Big Brother or Big Sister, or befriending an older person who does not drive.

Sometimes singles forget about family members: nieces, cousins, and uncles, whose very familiarity can make them ideal companions, allowing us to just be ourselves—not having to play games.

Hobbies and special interests are often a source of mutual activity with people. Sherry had decided that creating stained-glass objects would be her major hobby. While taking classes and building herself a well-supplied work area in her garage, she found a number of enthusiasts to share her interest in classes and at home. Jane joined the Sierra Club, faithfully attended hikes, and eventually worked up to an officer position in the group. She found companionship among the regulars with whom she hiked.

We can take advantage of singleness by establishing friendships with several different persons or groups who share our various interests: a weekly tennis game with Cliff, a monthly movie with Jan, a biweekly coffee with Sue from work. For many of us, leaving these get-togethers to spontaneity means that we will miss them because we forget to call or are too tired or too timid to make the effort. It takes energy to initiate; when we feel down or lonely, we do not have that energy. So when we have been with someone we enjoy and it seems to be mutual, it saves energy to establish the next meeting time before parting, and eventually to have a scheduled time and place to meet. Active singles find this energy-conserving framework valuable.

Companionship: A Summary

Companionship is being with people who occupy nearby space or share interests. Since companionship is a family feeling—not characterized by eros—the age, sex, or race of a companion does not matter as long as the two or more are at ease in each other's presence. The activity may be chatting, working silently, riding together, or pursuing a similar interest.

Establishing regular meeting times and places with groups or individuals creates stability in a single's life.

Companions may be only temporary and fit only one small dimension in our lives, or they may be family members or longtime friends for whom we also develop loyalty. When our lives shift, some temporary companions will naturally drop off. A wise person discerns when to let go of a temporary companion without feeling guilt—just thanksgiving for the enjoyment of lives temporarily touching.

---

1. What are the kinds of companionships you have observed or found helpful?
2. How could you combine service and companionship?

The Mind-Friend

Friendship of the mind—that exciting linking of thoughts that only happens intensely to a small percentage of people—

is not necessary for life, but it is the basis of creativity, the deep excitement available to people who are not currently occupied with survival and have not succumbed to the mind-blanking of spectator entertainment.

The difference between a companion and a mind-friend is that a companion's value is in his or her presence, whereas the mind-friend's value is in the ideas he or she stimulates through conversation. Mind-friends differ from intimates in that the focus of intimates is on feelings and personal growth rather than on ideas they hold in common. Spouses may be intimates without being mind-friends, because their topics of conversation may be themselves and their common activities and interests but not ideas.

Mind-friends differ from social friends because mind-friends may be so focused on ideas held in common that events like birthdays, car breakdowns, and other physical interruptions to the world of ideas seem insignificant. Men and women at work, pursuing hobbies, or on a project together may never ask about each other's personal life because it is irrelevant to the ideas the group is focusing on.

Mind-friends are persons who mentally click with each other, where the flow of conversation could go on forever because it is flowing in the same channel. Mind-friends are not exclusive since other persons with the same mindsets simply add to the stimulation of ideas. A person of a different mind, however, can entirely halt the momentum. Mind-friends are exclusive only in likeness of mind, which is necessary if ideas are to flow. Great discoveries in every field can be traced to a group of friends who were stimulated by mental interaction, because major creativity often arises from interactions of mind-friends.

A guide on the Acropolis in Athens tells of that friendship that existed among the great thinkers at the time of Athen's glory. They gathered frequently at the home of a woman to discuss ideas, even though they represented differing fields such as math, medicine, and philosophy. The writings of Plato are the kind of product that can come from mind-friends.

A small group of people concerned with mission in their church have met for discussion and prayer for the past year, resulting in the linking of old programs in the church with new ideas and strength. Alone, none of them would have initiated new projects, but strength has come through discussing ideas until they feel consensus and power to move.

Being a mind-friend is not limited to singles, of course, but one of the joys of singleness is the freedom to pursue friendships with people of like mind. Many people do not marry someone of like mind, since marriage is primarily for comfort rather than mental stimulation, so some marrieds who are into too much togetherness find themselves mentally stifled. Singles who seek mind-friends before marriage can be aware of the need for this freedom to continue, since it is a separate dimension from eros.

C. S. Lewis, in his book *The Four Loves* (Harcourt Brace Jovanovich, 1960), describes this kind of friendship as "the least natural of loves; the least instinctive, organic, biological, gregarious and necessary." He states that, "Without Eros none of us would have been begotten and without Affection [companionship] none of us would have been reared; but we can live and breed without Friendship [mind-friends]." Having mind-friends is a stimulating addition to one's life, not necessary for survival, but enjoyable, and necessary to the full creativity of which we are capable.

Another enriching element of mind-friends for singles is that this is one kind of male-female relationship that can provide the desirable man-woman dimension to one's life without the complications of eros. In eros, we look into each other's eyes as we do in intimacy; in long-term agape (loyalty), we look at each other's needs, a situation that could slip into eros if our minds declared the other person an eligible lover; in companionship, our eyes focus on a common activity, hence the chance of unwanted eros is decreased; but in mind-friend, the eyes are so focused on ideas, and the mind is so completely engaged, that this is the safest of activities for singles with marrieds of the opposite sex. Danger is still nearby since uncontrolled minds can always shift from ideas to fantasy, but for responsible, disciplined people, these relationships can be wonderfully rewarding.

150

Mind-friends, although not necessary for living, are necessary for the full development of ourselves as human beings. Each mind-friend brings out parts of us that will lie dormant without the germination that comes from the interaction with that particular mind. One mind-friend does not suffice to let us know ourselves or our potential. It is only in pursuing our interests and taking time to engage in idea-oriented conversations with a number of others that we begin to touch the possibilities of what God intended us to be.

Intimacy and Soul-Mates

The word *intimacy* is often associated with sex, but physical intimacy and personal or emotional intimacy are not synonymous. Even though personal intimacy can be communicated nonverbally through touch, eye contact, and caring actions that evidence special knowledge, the intimacy that reveals the inner self must be verbal. Our motives, dreams, hurts, and secret triumphs can only be known through words, since none of us can read minds or hearts.

The ultimate intimacy that anyone can experience is God in us, since his indwelling Spirit knows our every thought, action, motive, and desire. Though we can never know him as he knows us, he wants us to know him, having revealed himself to us through his actions, his creation, and his Word. With his total openness as a pattern, we can consider levels of intimacy humans can have with each other. Unlike God, we feel that we must hide, fearing that our inner self is unacceptable—too boring or too shameful for anyone else to accept and treasure. So we build walls to protect ourselves from the rejection we fear, and the walls keep us from intimacy.

Sharing honest desires and fears with God in prayer while another trusted person listens can be a deep kind of closeness—not only with God, but also with the other person, if both share openly. So prayer of this kind can become a vehicle of intimacy for people who are able to pray with honesty of feeling. To many Christians, prayer is a ritual with proper words to say, but with so much self-consciousness that intimacy never occurs. Only those who can lose themselves in God's love are able to experience this intimacy. Prayer partners can be two men, two women, or small groups of the same sex or mixed if they develop the trust that allows one soul to feel open to another.

Another level of intimacy is available to persons who can trust another human to accept the questionable parts of themselves. Once one has revealed one's darkest secret to one other person and been accepted—or even heard some respected person confess to the same or a worse secret—one is free to believe that intimacy is possible. The degree of trust determines the degree of intimacy in any relationship. But how does one learn this intimacy of soul, this deep friendship of sharing one's inner self?

Relating intimately takes mutual sharing of feelings, hopes, fears, joys, laughter, experiences, dreams, and memories over a period of time. Those who dare to be intimate suffer through the fear of rejection, the fear of appearing foolish, and the hesitancy of needing to check the other person's reaction on a later occasion after the mood of intimacy has passed.

Those who are successful in building the necessary trust are ones who never betray that trust by sharing it with someone else or by using the information as a weapon or as a joke. For those whose trust is betrayed but who risk continuation of the friendship, intimacy can be renewed by the betrayer who says "I'm sorry" and makes a new commitment to loyalty. Men and women are sometimes sensitive to different issues, causing misunderstandings if the friend does not realize that the information is classified. A woman almost lost a male companion by telling a mutual friend why he was in the hospital. It did not occur to the woman that the illness was secret, but many men feel private about their health. Men usually feel betrayed when women report personal conversations with their male friends to a female friend or prayer group. Women's openness and disloyalty (as interpreted by men) can cause men to retreat even more into a nonsharing role.

In our society, intimacy is expected among women, who

learn early that sharing feelings, fears, and hopes is acceptable, but some men never experience personal intimacy. Men have golf buddies and work friends, but it is rare to find them sharing inner struggles because our society teaches men to be strong, to protect themselves, to not cry. Men often do not even possess the language to identify a feeling in order to share it. They are taught to say "I think . . . " instead of "I feel . . . ." They may be able to talk about their anger (an acceptable emotion for males), but seldom about their joy, or disappointment (feelings identified as more feminine). If they talk about frustration, they often talk about what the other guy did, not about the inner conflict that actually frustrates. Their hopes are often expected to be tangible—money-oriented, or position-oriented goals—not what they want to be as humans, how they want to change, what kinds of relationships they desire, or how they are feeling about their current friendships.

Sex is another barrier to intimacy for singles since uncommitted men and women involved in sex have motives they feel are best not shared with their sex partners. Many notions in our society actually encourage men and women to pretend in matters of sex. For example, playing hard-to-get and making the partner jealous are methods supposed to increase interest, but they are opposed to sharing one's real feelings. Fear of losing a relationship, personal gratification, and the desire to manipulate are some motives for becoming involved sexually. These feelings cannot be safely shared with the partner, although they may be shared with another intimate. The high stakes of sex without commitment can make honest sharing risky.

Surprisingly, some single men find that their closest friends, those they can share with most intimately, may be their ex-spouses or old girlfriends after the hurt is over, sex and money issues have been settled, and both agree on the limitations of their relationship. Here are two persons who know each other well, have similar backgrounds, and have no need to keep secrets now that they are not trying to manipulate each other. Ironically, they may share feelings more honestly as friends than they ever did as a couple.

153

Intimacy and growth can be experienced by establishing one relationship, preferably with a peer of the same sex with whom we share our dreams, joys, edge of growth, and frustrations and to whom we confess our faults. I suggest a peer because a big difference in age or maturity often means sharing is not equal. An unequal relationship helps the less mature to grow and is delightful to the more mature as a mentor-learner ministry, but it does not stretch either person's risk-quotient as much as a peer relationship does. I suggest the same sex because we can understand our own sex in a way that we do not usually understand the other, although intimate heterosexual relationships can produce growth. No matter how deep the intimacy, honesty and reality arise when two talk to each other aware that God is listening, or talk to God about each other with the knowledge that the other is listening—in other words, when they honestly pray together.

Although we may think that sharing deeply is spontaneous, the situation that promotes depth can be programmed. A relationship that maintains depth, especially the kind of sharing that promotes personal growth, needs maintenance weekly or biweekly. If we are to grow into mature and healthy individuals, we need to establish an environment in which this sharing can easily occur. Time scheduled with a friend or a small group of friends all equally trusted can be divided into a time for each to share meaningful happenings of the past week and a time to affirm each other in prayer. Each person or group with whom one shares may be slightly different—some may focus on ministry, some on family, some on personal growth—but any trustful sharing is a reflection of God's life in us.

Many people would love to have a deeper intimacy in their lives, but are afraid to initiate. One approach to deepening a relationship is to catch a time when the mood is slow and the feeling is close, then to share a feeling or experience that exposes something vulnerable about oneself. The other may need prompting to share back, such as, "What's been your experience along this line?" Careful listening is what keeps the door to intimacy open. Silence, a change of subject, a laugh, and advice are all guaranteed to squelch further exchanges of a personal nature, pushing the relationship right back to the superficial, or perhaps ending the embryonic friendship entirely.

The knowledge that someone knows us deeply, still accepts us, and is willing to share our concerns is stabilizing. Singles can experience this personal intimacy by making themselves vulnerable, listening thoughtfully while others risk, and carefully guarding the vulnerability of their intimates.

Male-Female Friends

Since men and women think differently and approach life differently, we need male-female interaction in order to maintain a balanced understanding of life.

Last spring I was struck by a contrast in conversation, laughter, and atmosphere at two conferences I attended— the first composed of women, and the second a small group of singles, half men and half women. The presence of men created more joking, laughter, and a broader conversational base. Although the group knew each other well and no one was coupled or trying to impress anyone else, we women became more playful and softer when men were around. Even when we interact with members of the opposite sex who are not eligible to be partners for us, we still enhance each other's wholeness.

As more people over thirty-five become single because of divorce, and since men and women enjoy each other's company, friendships between men and women are increasing. At a party I attended recently, I observed that in more than half of the people over thirty-five attending as couples, the man was five to twenty years younger than the woman. Most of these were friends rather than potential lovers, because, when marriage isn't the primary goal, friendships between men and women of all ages are appropriate and enjoyable.

Singles become friends with married couples. Sometimes a friendship can occur between a single man and the wife or a single woman and the husband if the marriage is very stable, the spouse agrees, and the motivation in the married-single friendship is clearly not eros. With mature and honest families and singles who have celibate minds, these friendships can enrich all concerned, although they can be dangerous for the immature, the insecure, or if either has eros on the mind. Jesus made it clear in Matthew 5:28 that adultery in the mind is sin; he calls us to a celibate mind. A single participating in friendship with someone else's spouse is responsible for being certain that the relationship in no way interferes with the marriage. A Christian single's responsibility to God and to the friend is to honor the marriage vow above the friendship, since the priority of the marriage is unquestionable.

Somewhere among young and old acquaintances, co-workers, relatives, and neighbors are possibilities for male-female friendships that can enhance both partners. We will enrich ourselves if we take the time to nurture some of these.

---

1. How is it helpful to recognize the differences between companions, mind-friends, and soul-mates?

2. How have you developed soul-mates, prayer partners, or intimate friends?

3. Why is it all right to have some friends whose birthdays you do not remember or children's names you do not know?

4. Why is it important to have several friends meeting different needs rather than look for all friendship needs to be met in one person?

5. If the idea of mind-friends interests you, think of a class, committee, or activity you could attend in order to find someone of like mind.

6. Whom could you ask to be a prayer partner?

10

A HEALTHY SINGLE BUILDS A BASE CAMP

*S*ingleness can be very enjoyable, with a little planning.

Since most singles expect to get married, many ignore building relationships and structuring time to meet their affectional-belonging needs as singles. Focusing relational time on searching for Mr. or Ms. Right rather than on building an emotional base camp of friendships and activities has several negative consequences. First, these singles become too emotionally needy to choose wisely, since their affectional-belonging needs are not being adequately met. Therefore, they deplete themselves of the discernment necessary to select an appropriate mate, not seeing the possible mate as he or she really is, but rather seeing how much the other is meeting their immediate needs.

Second, having built no base of support through ongoing friendships or group activities, these singles are more vulnerable to depression during the "between" periods when one relationship has ended and another is not yet in sight. In addition, singles always on the search are primarily focused on their own needs and are seldom willing to make a commitment to serving others in any way that may interfere with the freedom to pursue the search for a future mate, thus limiting their growth into wholeness. Building an emotional base camp is essential to living wholesomely while one is single, and it provides a stronger base for marriage.

M. Scott Peck, in *The Road Less Traveled,* compares marriage with a base camp in mountain climbing. He emphasizes the necessity of carefully tending the base camp in order to venture up the peak of the mountain. The metaphor also points out that marriage is not an end in itself, not the goal, but one way to establish a social-emotional base from which to venture forth to fulfill one's meaning in life. Singles, by awareness of the components necessary for stability and joy in living, can also build a network of relationships as a support system that meets these needs for affection and belonging that all humans have. Even if one is only temporarily single, a base camp is vital to singleness and can continue to be a meaningful part of one's support system after marriage.

Abraham Maslow's hierarchy of needs (illustrated below)

expresses the idea that people tend to focus on the lowest level of need that is unfulfilled. For example, if a person is experiencing a marvelously stimulating conversation with an exciting person and a violent earthquake starts, both individuals will immediately become concerned with safety because it is a more basic need than affection or stimulating ideas. When safety is assured, the two can resume their pursuit of needs higher on the hierarchy. People concerned with poverty, safety, pain, or hunger are not usually concerned with esoteric ideas that the physically and emotionally satisfied person may find pleasurable.

In examining Maslow's hierarchy in relation to singles in our culture, we find that the top levels (self-actualization and esteem) and the bottom levels (physiological and safety) are unrelated to marriage. All survival needs, achievement needs, and self-actualization needs can be successfully met without marriage. This is illustrated by the fact that some women are even leaving marriages in order to fulfill themselves, feeling stifled in their pursuit of personal development in the role of wife.

Physical survival (including safety), financial survival (food, shelter, investments, retirement), and social survival (even social status for women) are now obtainable by a single. Marriage may be an easier route to accomplish some basics, but not too many people marry today solely for survival needs. Men can cook or eat out, and women can earn a living.

The needs just above survival but before achievement and self-actualization, social needs, are our stumbling blocks as singles. We still look to marriage as the main source of comfort, affection, and belonging. Finding one person to be the primary well from which we draw love and acceptance seems much easier than establishing a series of relationships that will provide emotional security. But in the long run, singles are healthier with a multiple-person base, and the potential satisfaction is greater for the single who has built varied meaningful relationships.

What does it take to establish a base camp? Marriage provides a structure that singles, especially those living alone, must build into their lives in order to obtain strength to reach out. Some elements of this framework are ritual, companionship, belonging, loyalty, intimacy, touch, and structuring of time.

Although all of these might possibly be met in one person, the secret of satisfying singleness is in separating out the strands of one's needs and cultivating specific relationships to meet each one. Even being single for a year is more comfortable if one is aware of these needs; and every change of residence or friendships necessitates rebuilding part of the structure.

One of the simple joys of life is to recognize each person we know as a gift from God by giving thanks for the particular pleasure that person brings to our lives, and by not expecting what that person is either unwilling or unable to give. Our fantasies of what relationships (especially male-female friendships) should be often deprive us of the joy of what they actually are—a unique friendship, companionship, or affection that may not fit any fantasy or common category. Each person, especially those in our inner circles, is a special gift to be enjoyed.

Ritual

The familiarity of a ritual in family life is comforting. A considerable part of family conversation is made up of greetings and trite comments. These words provide comfort because of the familiarity and lack of effort with which they are said, often becoming soothing oil on which relationships glide. Singles who are out of the habit of ritual greetings at home sometimes carry their silence into the world and miss the exchanges that smooth the flow of people.

Although with some people we exchange the same words day after day, the giving and receiving of a smile and affirmation lifts us and them. Singles need these familiar words with their housemates, neighbors, coworkers, or phone friends as a dependable pattern of life and to form the framework of humanness. Establishing routine so that we exchange pleasantries daily with a few persons affirms our place as social beings and helps our minds stay productive. Traditions and habits such as watching certain games with friends, getting season tickets with old friends, continuing holiday customs with family or groups help to maintain balance and meaning in life.

For retired, handicapped, or self-employed people who do not have a regular work ritual, establishing routines is even more important. Many widows arrange a daily call at a certain time with another widow as a safety factor in case of illness or accident. The calls also provide a sounding board for the continuing saga of life, which we all need to share with someone in order to feel human. People without a regular reporting partner often overwhelm listeners when they do find an opportunity to talk, squeezing the occasion until the trapped listener struggles to escape.

Although some singles resist the superficiality of mundane, predictable responses to repetitive situations, ritual provides a rhythm and familiarity to living that comforts us. It forms the fabric of life on which meaningful relationships and achievements appear as colorful embroidered designs. Without these routine exchanges, we tend to withdraw into a nonperson role.

For persons living alone, especially those without the regular routine of work, having a pet animal can provide routine that contributes to productive living. The animal's need for meals and love makes demands on us that keep us responsible and functional. Routine and being needed keep our energy levels up, and animals can help in this for those who choose to live alone.

We need the familiar, the predictable, the kind of love C. S. Lewis calls *storge* in *The Four Loves*. We need friends who are aware of our comings and goings, who observe the patterns of our lives, who miss us if we skip the coffee break or don't buy the morning paper. Since our basic humanness depends on some kind of response from other humans, we need to build ritual into our lives.

Belonging

In God's plan of family structure, the extended family (grandparents, aunts, uncles, et al.) also has a role. We all need more than one person to belong to; we need a clan, a group. Identity, protection, companionship that is safe because the roles are predetermined, rituals for holidays, and major life events are given structure by extended families. Many singles and marrieds who have left their home towns or whose families have dispersed find themselves needing to create places to belong.

In old-fashioned families a person is accepted because of birth into the clan and regardless of personality quirks, disabilities, or performance. We all long for that total acceptance without any effort on our part, but in reality we must all find or form our own groups, many of them short-term because we cannot predict the future or command

161

anyone else's performance, but, it is to be hoped, one or two that may last a lifetime and be a true substitute family.

Some singles adopt a friend's family and feel accepted, or some form groups from work, church, the neighborhood, or their former high school or college friends. The groups that last are those that agree upon a meeting time, are formed around a common interest or feeling of family, and have enough proximity that the effort to get together is not inhibiting. Since married people also need groups for belonging beyond the nuclear family, some of the healthiest groups often include both singles and those married.

Activity groups in church, on the job, and for volunteer projects also provide a sense of belonging because membership is clear-cut and the purpose establishes self-worth. Committees, boards, and missions to accomplish certain objectives all have the potential to provide a sense of belonging. Everyone who has been chosen to be on a committee or board has a right to be there, so one does not experience the uncertainty that may arise in social groups where acceptance is not predetermined. The purpose of the committee probably indicates common interests that may also extend to friendships outside the group. So joining committees or volunteering for work projects can fulfill two needs—belonging and self-worth.

God designed us to be in community by making us members of the body of Christ at the same time we became united with Christ. Although some Christians don't act out this union in life, trying to live their faith independent of God's community, this is blasphemous to God's design for their lives. Many who look for the sense of belonging in the church, however, find that the impersonalness of the worship service does not provide the oneness they seek. Becoming a member of a class, small group, or Bible study is usually necessary to feel that sense of belonging in the church. But even if a person does not find that feeling in the worship service, corporate worship is a spiritual reality that is part of God's plan for Christians, and he will honor those who follow his design.

Many cults use a technique called "love bombing," which quickly absorbs newcomers into the group by surrounding them with love. The human need for belonging is great, and healthy singles must choose their places of belonging in groups that will benefit their growth into whole persons. We must also help other, less capable loners find belonging in healthy places.

One of the advantages of singleness is the freedom to come and go as we please without consulting anyone. The flip side of that advantage is that singles may find it difficult to make commitments. Christian singles need commitment to a church, and they need a commitment to serve in some responsible way in that church. Singles in the "search pattern" find it more desirable to stay uncommitted in order to go where the most exciting activity may be, but lack of commitment decreases one's belonging, fulfillment, and ability to serve responsibly. Therefore, committing oneself to one church for identity and service is a way to meet this basic need for belonging that we have.

We all identify with certain people as being "my kind of people." We each have, in addition to that imprinting that tells us what our "other half" should be like, a recognition of those persons who could be "family." As we meet individuals with whom we feel an emotional bond, we recognize that these could be our nephews, aunts, brothers, or cousins. They feel like family in their sense of humor or values, their interests or mannerisms, and sometimes in their physical makeup. We identify these people by an awareness of attraction, a feeling of being at home in their presence, of being able to share a raised eyebrow or knowing look even in early stages of acquaintance. Although this feeling may have the potential to develop into eros in some cases, if we identify these people as family rather than lovers and join with them in groups rather than just one-on-one, we can let ourselves thoroughly enjoy being attracted to people of all ages and races, both sexes, married or single. And when we identify them, we need to find some way to include them in a group with us. Have a work party; ask to include them in a friend's get-together; arrange to meet several at a restaurant for lunch; invite a few to drop by for soup, meet for tennis, for church, go to a game—anything to increase the sense of belonging.

We each are responsible to find or form some groups that we attend regularly enough and participate in wholeheartedly enough that we will be missed if we are not there. If we aren't missed, we need to evaluate the choice of group and the quality of our participation until we find those groups in which we are able to make an acceptable contribution, and in which the interaction is as meaningful to the other members as to us. Blaming other people for not including us serves no purpose except to isolate us further. We are responsible for finding those who consider us "their kind of people."

---

1. What is a support base for singles?
2. How is ritual helpful in life?
3. What are your circles of belonging? Are you overextended or underextended, and how can this be remedied?

Loyalty

New singles, young singles, and mobile singles tend to have a continuing flow of new friends. Many of us can look back two or three years and realize that none of the people we were close to several years ago is currently our friend. Some moved, some married, our interests changed, or we simply have no reason to keep in touch with friends of the past. Stimulating as this kind of freshness may be, it also lends a disjointedness to life that leaves us without continuity or people we can count on when needs arise.

Although knowing that there is someone who can be counted on in times of trouble is quite basic to our stability, we cannot demand that loyalty—not from family, and not from friends. Since loyalty generally comes from longevity, keeping in touch with some family members or longtime friends has great value—even if current interests do not match as well as they once did. Closeness ebbs and flows depending on current events in one's life, but what a joy to have those persons, even distant, with whom there is immediate caring, interest, and sharing when contact is made.

Two factors may help establish dependable relationships. First, we can show loyalty to family and friends by remembering birthdays, sending cards or gifts, answering letters, making phone calls, responding to announcements and invitations, listening to their hurts and sorrows, giving help, and being aware of need. However, being loyal does not guarantee loyalty in return. Second, accept loyalty as a gift from God from whoever offers it. The angels he chooses to deliver his mercy may not be the persons we desired to be our faithful friends, but appreciating and reciprocating loyalty is fundamental to our personal strength.

Humans Need Touch

Our society gives approval to touch between humans in limited areas: family life, sports, medical needs, and certain grooming needs. Singles may be lacking in touch if they have no small children, no recurring medical needs, are not involved in contact sports, and take care of their own grooming. Many articles have been written recently about the need our bodies have for physical contact with other humans. According to these articles, the "hug quotient" seems to range from five to forty a day for healthy living. Lack of touch seems to bring on an emotional irritability that is generally recognizable; for example, when men say about a grumpy woman, "She needs a good man," meaning a man in bed. Sex provides touch, but it is not the only source. Singles who are abstainers need to find alternative means of giving and receiving touch, which is a necessary ingredient of physical and emotional health.

Most abstainers find it uncomfortable to become sexually aroused without fulfillment, so the caressing, which is sexual

165

foreplay, does not answer this need satisfactorily. Those whose work or social life brings them together with children can be healthy contributors to children's needs and their own by reading a book together or playing sports with them. Some people are comfortable giving or receiving a hand on the arm while in conversation, while others shake hands with everyone they meet.

Hugs are controversial in many places, but are an ideal way to meet the need for touch where they are acceptable. In some churches men are free to hug men, pastors are free to hug parishioners, women can hug women, and even men and women can hug in greeting while the church is looking on. At the end of each worship service in the First Presbyterian Church of Hollywood, worshipers who come forward for prayer with the elders receive prayer with the laying on of hands, which is a warm and healing experience.

Some friends in our lives have a healing effect on us from their physical presence. Linking arms or hands with them while walking across the street, leaning shoulder to shoulder in the coffee shop booth, or simply sitting close in conversation can have a soothing effect.

Soothing, also, are professional contacts such as shampoos, coiffures, pedicures, manicures, massages, and chiropractic treatments. Many widows have their hair done weekly, not only for the morale boost in looking good and the social contact that women find in beauty shops, but also for the soothing effect the beautician's fingers have on their hair and scalp. Professional grooming care for someone living alone and with limited means of touch is well worth the money in both physical and emotional health.

A wonderful gift that some people have is the skill of massage. One woman, who is expert at easing tension by massaging, delights her friends by easing all the tension from their necks and shoulders in a few minutes with her skilled fingers. Another woman, hunched over a typewriter trying to finish some work for a male friend, was pleased when he thoughtfully rubbed her neck. That neckrub almost ended in bed. Massaging can be sexually stimulating or it can be a generous gift of comfort.

166

So we have a choice: we can eliminate all back-rubbing because sometimes it can be sexually stimulating, or we can learn to know our own bodies' signals and read the signals of others to be able to stop at appropriate points. The woman who eases her friends' shoulder tensions sometimes gives shoulder massages to her dates. Recognizing where massaging can lead and wanting to stay celibate at this point in her life, she is very careful to keep her massaging below the stimulus level of arousal. However, this gift provides a feeling of closeness and an atmosphere that is conducive to personal sharing in conversation.

Touch is a wonderful gift that we can give each other. We need to build into our lives ways to give and receive physical contact with others to keep us from being irritable.

Developing Routines

Persons living in families have some established routines that provide a structure for living. Usually, they eat at least one meal a day together and bump into each other around the house in familiar patterns. People living alone also form routines, but planning these routines to include friends on a regular basis helps singles to be more fully human. We need to include friends in our daily routines, in our weekly and monthly schedules, and in our seasonal and yearly planning.

Establishing someone in our lives with whom we share daily happenings, someone who knows the people and continuing events that make up our particular history, someone who knows where we have gone and when to expect us back provides continuity. The relationship doesn't have to be deep—just someone to whom we can say, "Mother's coming to visit, Sally's upset with me, and I finally got the car dent fixed": the mundane of life, yet the continuing saga that makes up most of living. It is valuable to have individuals to whom we can speak shorthand because they know the people and current events in our lives; having to explain everything again and again is draining. Since much humor comes from shared knowledge, old friends are usually worth the effort to maintain even though during some periods of time our interests diverge. Many singles who live alone establish a daily phone contact to fill this basic function; for some it's the coffee break, while some meet after work for socializing or for a meal. Daily continuity of life must be arranged if we are to feel wholly human.

Next are the weekly and monthly routines that ensure that we are balancing our lives with service, intimacy, male-female interaction, and individuals and groups with whom we can pursue our interests and have fun. Herein we balance our time for solitude and socializing, pleasure and service, and creative and mundane activities in the way that will best move us toward wholeness at this point in our lives.

Planning for the future is a fearful concern for some singles because they are waiting for a spouse. Fear of becoming too defined, too independent, or fear of not being available for a spouse inhibits some singles from making long-term commitments for a job, for buying property, or for a ministry that may limit social life because of time or travel. The more wholly a person lives by planning whatever seems appropriate, even if it has to be changed later, the more one has to offer a relationship. Fear and holding back from experiencing one's current (wholesome) desires in order to save the experience to have with some future spouse can shrivel a person. We need to plan our lives as individuals, wholly with all of the persons currently in our lives, willing to commit ourselves to plans that will enhance our wholeness. Flexibility means willingness to change as circumstances change—with honesty and consideration for those in the old plans—not lack of planning or the tentativeness that no one can count on.

Holidays need to be planned by singles since "family" times of the year can trigger loneliness. Increasingly, singles are establishing traditions of their own for the holidays. Some regularly hold an open house on Christmas or New Year's Day while others invite a select group for dinner, tree-decorating, Christmas caroling, or brunch.

This past year the singles at the First Presbyterian Church of Hollywood served two hundred street people Thanksgiving dinner in the church hall and nearly five hundred people at Christmas. These singles spent their day—and several days before for some—cooking, waiting tables, hosting, and cleaning up. Singles expressed great satisfaction in the fellowship of working together and serving others.

Planning vacations and traveling with continuing friends provides more enjoyment because of shared planning before and memories after.

Time structuring can eliminate loneliness when one knows oneself well enough to plan appropriately. Evaluating one's needs and planning activities for different purposes enables a single to enjoy life more fully.

---

1. Is hugging accepted in the groups you are in? What are alternative ways of giving and receiving touch?

2. How do you maintain contact with long-term friends or relatives?

3. How do you express loyalty in your close relationships?

4. In what areas is your time best appropriated? What areas do you need to work on?

===11===

A HEALTHY SINGLE
FINDS MEANING

Many singles and those married spend their entire lives working on the middle levels of the hierarchy of needs: social and esteem needs. But for those whose base camps are in order, satisfaction comes from working on the higher level—self-actualization. Aspects of personal development that Christian singles find meaningful include fulfillment through developing their gifts, finding God's purpose, and enjoying the risk of adventure. The following sections will describe how these options work for singles.

What Is Fulfillment?

Fulfillment is being a total participant in God's purpose for our lives. His purpose includes receiving all of his love for us, giving it back to him, giving love to the people around us, developing and using the gifts he has given us, and ministering with him to all the creatures and creation.

We may achieve many things in our lives and yet develop few of our gifts. Being all that God intends us to be may mean developing our natural talents, which may have nothing to do with the way we make a living, and it does mean exploring for our spiritual gifts, of which we may not even be aware. Using our gifts will result in ministries and missions that will utilize who we are and put us in relationships that will bring us amazing fulfillment.

Another advantage of singleness is the freedom for adventure. Instead of playing the waiting game, thinking that life does not begin until marriage, we have the

170

opportunity to utilize our time for trying options we might never attempt after being tied down by marriage.

What Fulfillment Is Not

Fulfillment is not sex or lack of sex, since the sex act in itself does not bring personal fulfillment, nor does the lack of sexual intercourse prevent us from fulfillment. Momentary pleasure and fulfillment are two quite different experiences.

Fulfillment is not self-indulgence. The focus on finding "the one" is self-indulgent, as are all the ways we comfort ourselves—spending money on an excess of clothing, jewelry, household frivolities, entertainment, or cars, or by spending our time excessively on pleasure and comforts, for example. Indulging our wants, like indulging in sex, can bring momentary pleasure, but too much focus on our own satisfaction decreases the pleasure and keeps us from focusing on the risk that real fulfillment calls for.

Fulfillment is not trying to follow a human-made time chart of what the good life or the God-directed life should look like: marry a certain perfectly matched spouse at a given time, have children at the right time, do well in a satisfying career, gain recognition, and have funds for retirement. When God doesn't come through on the prescribed timeline, we figure that he doesn't keep his promises or that we are unworthy, forgetting that God's timing is often completely different from ours—consider Abraham beginning to follow God's call at seventy-five, Moses at eighty, Sarah delivering her first child at ninety, Jesus dying at thirty-three, Stephen stoned to death perhaps even younger than that. God's goals also are often different, since his plan for us is to build character whereas ours is quite often to find happiness, fulfillment, or "the good life."

Elements of Fulfillment

No one finds fulfillment without being involved in ministry. Since singles have greater choice in their commitments of time, they can choose to develop their potential gifts and ministries as far as they want. At whatever stage of development we are, as we use all that we know and risk growth, we find fulfillment. As soon as we try to stay on some plateau that is already familiar, we lose the adventure, and dullness sets in.

None of us has time in this life to develop all gifts, but if we respond to those desires that arise—to take piano lessons, to learn Hebrew, to get out the paint set—without worrying that it is too late, or that we will never become the best, we can nurture some of what God has given us. And as we develop our knowledge and creativity, we expand our likeness to God, the omniscient Creator.

Likewise, spiritual gifts are only developed by using them, and only known by following the promptings of the Spirit. When someone says, "Pray for me," why not risk saying, "Sure, how about now?" instead of diligently putting the name on a prayer list. When a need arises for calling, organizing, teaching, visiting, why not say, "I'll try." When we experiment and offer to go out of our way to serve, we discover and develop our spiritual gifts. Remember, spiritual gifts are given for the moment as the need arises—we miss out if we are not available to serve or will not risk new endeavors.

A special opportunity for fulfillment comes in the freedom to arrange for a quiet time with God. The choice to rise early or stay up late, to go off alone or sing and dance before God, to undergo a silence retreat or a fast, enhances our possibility of communion with God. Because others are not imposing a schedule on us, we may become lazy and use our time less wisely than those with fewer choices, but the opportunity to try out new experiences in contemplation and awareness of God is a wonderful gift, and we should take advantage of it.

Although marriage symbolizes the love of Christ for the church, a single reflects God's creation of each individual person. Marriage is temporary, lasting only in this life, while our individuality is eternal since we are born as individuals, are saved as individuals, die as individuals, and live through eternity in an unmarried state. We singles represent that personal relationship with God for which each person, male or female, is responsible.

Fulfillment is walking in the purposes that God has for humans, utilizing the resources of the indwelling Spirit, growing in the knowledge of and obedience to Scripture, and experiencing the support and responsibility of the body of believers. It is an attitude of mind that is open to the risk of living and loving to the fullest. Although marriage can bring comfort, some security, and a measure of satisfaction, deep fulfillment is unrelated to marriage and open to anyone willing to risk—risk the work and attention involved in loving, risk the vulnerability necessary for sharing and working toward one's dreams, and risk seeking forgiveness and trying again after one has failed.

Ready for Adventure

For those singles with solid base camps and rewarding friendships, adventure is the next option. God has promised to give us the desires of our hearts if we delight in him. When we move our focus away from finding a spouse or lover or satisfying our sex needs, we find many desires surfacing from our hearts into our minds. Part of our uniqueness is in the particular desires that emerge for us, whether artistic, humanitarian, performance-oriented, or organizational. Whatever the desire, pursuing it will be an adventure.

As singles, and especially as celibates who are not caught up in self-gratification, we are free to choose how to use our time, energy, and money. We are free to move, to quit our jobs for the risk of a business of our own, to work part-time in pursuit of a hobby or ministry, or to travel overseas.

Because some singles have been looking for a spouse for their entire adult and semi-adult lives, they have been afraid to go overseas, move to a small community, buy a house, or even commit themselves to teach a Sunday school class for an entire year because they might miss out on a possibility of marriage. Such a waste! If marriage is for the long-term single, it will happen in the midst of adventure or service or a new hobby. A person continually seeking a mate grows stagnant. When excitement comes into our lives, the blood flows faster, the body is energized, and marriage is no longer sought as the great panacea. When we are already risking adventure, we are more willing to risk relationships, making us more likely to develop friendships that are satisfying.

So on to adventure. There are many short-term assignments singles can take in other countries: the Peace Corps, teaching English for other governments or businesses overseas, missionary projects that last from a few months to a few years, work in almost any field one has training in. The church needs Christians living a life of love around the world. The American church needs Christians who have lived in other cultures if it is to see how Christianity is skewed by Americanism. The single is in a unique position to make this valuable contribution to Christ's kingdom.

Often in an overseas assignment, the community to which one can belong is limited in size to the extent one cannot escape or hide, which creates a marvelous opportunity to practice love. Since some singles have a propensity for wanting to escape, a commitment to such a community could be an opportunity to learn the art of love.

For those not desiring an adventure overseas, other cultures exist in our own cities that need our understanding and interest. International students and newcomers to our country can enrich our lives immensely while we show them hospitality. Telephone "lifelines" are in need of volunteer help for those who are willing to interact with people over the phone. Using one's own phone to encourage those tied at home or too shy to go out is a two-way adventure in human relationships. Whenever we step out into some activity that is a little scary, something we haven't yet conquered, we are risking adventure and expanding ourselves to become more whole human beings.

Those with the gift of hospitality can take in refugees, relatives, friends, and children of friends. The people-oriented can meet people for coffee, for meals, for a sporting event, or for a movie, since as singles we can usually make our time flexible if we choose.

Singles who are more idea-oriented or object-oriented may find the desires that surface, when they examine their hearts, to be dreams of performing, organizing, or programming. As we expose our dreams to our mind-friends, we will find encouragement and our visions will often jell and enlarge into even greater adventures. Our vision may be a mural to cover a wall of graffiti, a play to put on for the community, a potluck meal to bring people together. Whatever the dream, remember that God is the one who gives us our desires if our delight is in him, and therefore the dream needs to be exposed to our mind-friends, planned, and acted upon so that we can get on with the adventure of living and growing.

Some singles attempt to use sex as a substitute for adventure and the intimacy that comes from adventuring together. Sexual intercourse without true friendship and deep sharing does not impart intimacy. The adventure of the conquest soon becomes boring without a real relationship because it requires so much repetition. Real adventure for singles is in daring to let one's dreams surface and daring to expose them to those who can encourage the realization of their potential, then working with others in the joy of attempting to pull them off. Friendship through the shared adventure of working and serving together brings joy.

Men who have served in battle together sometimes find the war the highlight of their lives—not because of the war, but because of the intimacy of sharing death and almost death and fear of death together. Losing themselves in caring for their comrades and sharing with their comrades gave them a greater experience of intimacy than some have ever experienced again.

When people look back on the times of their lives that have been the most rewarding, they usually recall adventures with others in which a common purpose required them to move out of their security and step into the unfamiliar where risk and trust were necessary. Some have worked with a team of people on a job that binds them to their teammates in a demanding adventure of mind. Some have experienced fellowship in service projects that have walked the edge of adventure. Some have banded together for evangelism projects that are beyond their experience, requiring them to lean on God and stretch their abilities. The freedom to venture boldly into something we love doing, especially something that requires risk and bonds us to coadventurers, is the joy of being single.

If you are a long-term single who may be continuing in singleness indefinitely, rejoice in the adventure that is yours. Those expecting marriage should take advantage of this time for growth and exploration. You may never be as free again.

---

1. What have been the adventures in your life that have called forth your best?

2. What gifts or talents have you delayed developing, but still appeal to you?

3. What new risk in serving God and his world might be a next step for you?
